2 ⁰⁰

The Manual of
HORSEMANSHIP
of the British Horse Society and the Pony Club

1ST EDITION	.	1950
2ND EDITION	.	1954
3RD EDITION	.	1956
4TH EDITION	.	1959
REPRINTED	.	1960
5TH EDITION	.	1961
REPRINTED	.	1962
REPRINTED	.	1963
REPRINTED	.	1964
6TH EDITION	.	1966
REPRINTED	.	1967
REPRINTED	.	1968
REPRINTED	.	1969
REPRINTED	.	1969
REPRINTED	.	1970
REPRINTED	.	1970
REPRINTED	.	1971
REPRINTED	.	1972
REPRINTED	.	1976

THE BRITISH HORSE SOCIETY
KENILWORTH, WARWICKSHIRE, CV8 2LR

Published in 1976 by
BARRON'S
Woodbury, N.Y.

The publisher gratefully acknowledges the kindness of Educational Productions Limited, Wakefield, England in granting us permission to reproduce illustrations by Joan Wanklyn from the book *Play the Game Riding* by Mrs. V.D.S. Williams, as well as the kindness of Moss Bros. Limited of Covent Garden, London, England and of George Parker & Sons, London, England in granting us permission to reproduce the photographs of bits illustrated on pages 29 and 30.

Published in 1976 by
Barron's Educational Series, Inc.
113 Crossways Park Drive
Woodbury, N.Y. 11797

Paper Edition
International Standard Book No. 0-8120-0666-6

Case Bound Edition
International Standard Book No. 0-8120-5105-x

Library of Congress Catalog No. 76-8050

FOREWORD

This, the sixth, edition has been considerably revised and is recommended for use by members of the British Horse Society, the Pony Club, the Riding Clubs and by other associated organisations.

It covers, with "Training the Young Horse and Pony," the entire syllabus of the Pony Club and has the aim of laying the foundations for good, basic and effective horsemanship which can later be developed, as desired, into more specialised forms of riding. It is also applicable to those of more mature age.

It is based on the fundamental principles and practices of horsemanship which have stood the test of time; at the same time it follows modern thinking on equitation and training.

Because it is the recognised official Manual of the Pony Club it is not considered necessary to substitute the word "horse" for "pony" in all sections where either word is equally applicable. In instances where the pronouns *he* and *him* appear, they have been used to avoid awkward prose. It should be understood that these references apply to all riders, whether male or female.

Instructors are recommended to read "Training the Young Horse and Pony" and "The Instructors Handbook" in conjunction with this Manual.

The Pony Club and Riding Club Tests and the B.H.S. Instructors Examination are based on these books.

CONTENTS

Arrangement of this book.

The book is divided into three parts dealing with Equitation, Saddlery and Horsemastership.

Part I deals primarily with riding, the position of the rider and control of the horse or pony.

There follow two appendices about elementary dressage. Appendix I describes a system of training and Appendix II contains definitions of the various terms and movements. The appendices deal with more advanced riding and movements than the earlier sections of the book.

Part II deals with the fitting as well as with the care and cleaning of saddlery. It also describes how to put on and take off a saddle and bridle.

Part III includes the handling and care of horses and ponies at grass and in stables; also veterinary notes, the identification of horses and ponies and road transport.

The training of young horses and ponies is dealt with in a separate book "Training the Young Horse and Pony", also published by The British Horse Society.

An index will be found at the end of the book.

PART I. EQUITATION

CONTENTS

PART II. SADDLERY

CONTENTS

PART III. HORSEMASTERSHIP

CONTENTS

CONTENTS

CONTENTS

CONTENTS

CONTENTS

ILLUSTRATIONS

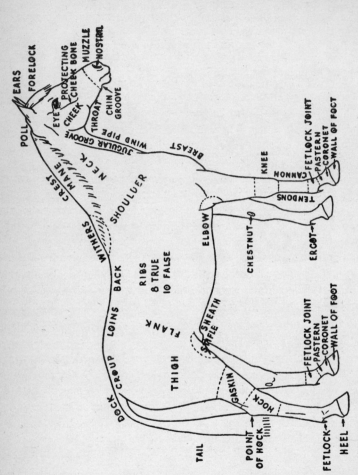

FIGURE 1. THE POINTS OF THE HORSE

xvi

PART I.

EQUITATION

MOUNTING AND DISMOUNTING

To mount from the near-side

See that the girths are tight and the stirrup irons down. Stand with the left shoulder to the horse's near shoulder and take the reins and stick in the left hand, the reins properly separated for riding and of a suitable length to prevent the horse from moving, with the off-side slightly shorter than the near. Place the left hand in front of the withers and, with the aid of the right hand, place the left foot in the stirrup. Press the toe down so as to come under the girth, pivot the body round to face the horse, seize the waist or the far side or the front arch of the saddle and spring lightly up. Swing the right leg over, taking care that the foot does not brush the horse's quarters, and at the same time move the hand from the rear to the front arch of the saddle, allowing the body to sink gently into the saddle without a bump. Place the right foot quietly in the stirrup and take up the reins.

To dismount on the near-side

Remove both feet from the stirrups. Lean forward, placing the left hand, with whip or stick, on the horse's neck. Place the right hand on the pommel of the saddle and vault off, keeping the right leg well clear of the horse's back. Be careful to land on the toes and avoid the horse's front legs. The right hand should then take hold of the reins close up to the bit.

Care should be taken to see that both feet are released from the stirrups before attempting to dismount. On no account must the legs be thrown over the horse's withers as during this time the reins would be dropped and control of the horse lost, so that any movement might cause a nasty fall on the back of the head.

To dismount on the near-side by using the stirrup

This alternative method is given but not recommended for general use. Accidents, etc., may necessitate its use. Take the reins and stick in the left hand and place the fingers of the left hand on the horse's mane. Take the front arch of the saddle with the right hand and at the same time quit the off-side stirrup iron. Pass the right leg over the horse's back and the right hand to the rear of the saddle. Then lower the right foot to the ground and remove the left foot from the stirrup. The weight of the body should be kept central until the right leg is clear of the horse's back.

Mounting and dismounting on the off-side should also be practised.

THE SEAT*

The seat means the rider's position in the saddle and the security and control over the horse that must accompany it.

A good seat is dependent upon a judicious combination of balance, suppleness and grip. The good horseman rides most of the time by balance and poise, with which rhythm is closely associated. His position in the saddle must be such that he can apply grip instantly to preserve balance *before* this is lost. Suppleness makes balance possible and perfects it.

A good saddle will assist the rider to sit with the seat in the centre and lowest part and will also allow for varying lengths of stirrup leathers to be used, without the seat being pushed back. Such a saddle is adequate for all forms of normal riding; but for race-riding, advanced dressage and advanced show jumping, special saddles may be required.

---

*NOTE: This subject is also covered by the Pony Club Film Strip Book, "The General Purpose Seat".

It is essential to acquire and maintain a good, strong seat, independent of any assistance from the reins. This is achieved by regular, active riding and can be assisted by the practise of suppling exercises. (See Physical Exercises on page 11.)

THE POSITION OF THE RIDER

The seat should be well down in the centre and lowest part of the saddle, the rider sitting square and level. The upper part of the body should be upright and free from all stiffness especially about the waist. Stiffness in one part of the body will produce muscular contraction in another. The head should be erect and the eyes looking between the horse's ears. The rider should be straight without being stiff and supple without appearing slack.

The knee and thigh should at all times be close to the saddle, with the large thigh muscles behind, so as not to lie between the saddle and the thigh bone. The natural grip thus formed by a correct knee and thigh position, must be downwards and inwards, and should not be unduly exerted, except in an emergency. The knee and ankle must be supple. Any stiffness in these joints will tend to make the upper part of the body stiff.

The lower part of the leg should be kept back and free to apply close behind the girth. It should hang lightly touching the horse's side with the stirrup leather vertical when on level ground. An incorrect position of the lower leg will upset the rider's balance, needing an alteration of the body to a faulty position to restore it.

The foot. The downward thrust on the stirrups will pass into the heels, causing them to sink below the level of the toes and allowing the ankle joints to flex freely with the movements of the horse. To this end the stirrup should usually be held on the ball of the foot; when occasion arises it will not be difficult to put the feet home in the stirrups. The foot should rest in a relaxed position

FIGURE 2.   THE POSITION OF THE RIDER

with the toe pointing generally towards the front. Toes turned out
to excess affect the proper contact of the knee with the saddle and
tend to encourage a grip with the calf. Toes turned in to excess
tend to stiffen the ankle and remove the calf from contact with the
horse's side.

The position of the knees and toes, being dictated by the position
of the whole leg from the hip joint, should be natural and not
forced.

The arms should hang naturally down to the elbows, which
should be lightly touching the sides. Viewed from the side, the

forearms should be in a straight line through the reins to the horse's mouth. The hands, with thumbs uppermost, will be just above and in front of the front arch of the saddle. The wrists and fingers should be supple and ready to follow every movement of the horse's head and neck. There should be no exaggerated rounding of the wrists.

THE LENGTH OF STIRRUP TO ADOPT

If a rider adopts a very long stirrup he will have a weak seat as there will be nothing to prevent him from being thrown or pulled forward. The only advantage will be the full use of the legs. If the stirrup is too short the rider's seat is pushed back so that the weight is on the horse's loins and the seat and leg aids cannot be effectively used.

The rider who adopts a short stirrup is less likely to be pulled forward, owing to having the full length of his thigh in front of him. The disadvantage of the short stirrup is the loss of use of the leg. It can be seen, therefore, that it is best to adopt a length of stirrup which gives as strong a seat as possible without hindering the use of the legs. This is the length generally adopted in the hunting field. See figure 2.

The pupil should learn to measure his correct length of leather by standing facing the saddle, placing the knuckles of the fingers of the right hand on the stirrup bar on the saddle and measuring the leather and iron under the arm. A good practical length will allow the iron to reach into the arm-pit.

It will be found that the beginner frequently rides with stirrups too short. This is because he is gradually working his way down in the saddle. It is a good idea to ride for a short time without stirrups. Then stretch down the legs and toes as far as they will go. After this, fit the stirrups again and it will be found that, in many cases, they have to be lengthened.

To lengthen or shorten stirrups

To alter the right stirrup, first take the reins in the left hand. With the right hand take hold of the spare end of the leather, and with the thumb on the top of the buckle, steer the tongue of the buckle with the first finger, the other three fingers holding the spare end of the leather; disengage the tongue and guide into the required hole, then move the buckle up close to the bar of the saddle by pulling down on the inside leather, and replace the end of the leather. The foot should *never* be removed from the stirrup. Riders should get into the habit of changing the length of their stirrups without looking down.

The position at the walk

The position of the upper part of the body does not alter except that it moves slightly in rhythm with the natural movement of the horse. The rider must look in the direction in which he is going.

The position at the trot

There are two ways of riding at the trot: "Sitting", when the seat should not leave the saddle; and "Rising" in the saddle. The former is used during transitions from one pace to another and on other occasions, when required. It enables the rider to remain in closer contact with his horse and not to lose contact if his mount tries to evade any of the aids.

The rising trot, when done correctly, is an easy motion for both horse and rider. The trot of a horse is an alternate movement of the two diagonals (a pace of two-time). The off-fore and the near-hind are the right diagonal, and the near-fore and the off-hind, the left diagonal. A rider is said to be riding on the right diagonal when his seat returns to the saddle as the horse's off-fore and near-hind come to the ground. The diagonal can be changed by sitting down in the saddle for an extra beat before commencing to rise again. The rider should change the diagonal when he changes the rein and at frequent intervals when hacking. In practically all cases, due to insufficient practice and lack of training, one diagonal appears to be more comfortable than the other. In the rising trot the movement should be smooth with no jerks or bumps. The upper part of the body should be inclined slightly forward and care taken not to thrust the seat back. The small of the back should be supple. There should be no effort on the part of the rider to rise in the saddle. The body should be placed in such a position that the horse is made to do all the work of throwing the body up. The movement should be assisted by the knees and ankle joints.

The main fault in trotting is trying to rise with a stiff and hollow back. This will mean that the stomach is pushed forward as the rider rises. In a bad case the effort is so great that the rider will resort to the reins in order to pull himself up.

The complete novice, however, will tend to get the body too far forward.

The position at the canter

The canter is a pace of three-time. In other words, there are three distinct beats to each stride.

At this pace the suppleness of the small of the back is most important. The upper part of the body should give to the motion and rhythm of the horse. The seat should remain well down in the saddle and should not appear to leave it.

One main fault is a stiff and rigid back, resulting in the seat bumping up and down in the saddle. Another is sitting on the fork with the weight too far forward off the seat bones, thus "driving the horse into the ground".

The position at the gallop

There are two alternative positions which may be adopted for riding at the gallop.

(1) When a horse requires driving, the rider should sit well down in the saddle and push the horse forward with his seat and legs.

(2) When a horse moves freely the rider should adopt a forward position. The weight of the body should be taken on the knees and stirrups. The weight of the seat should be off the saddle with the body leaning forward over the hands. As long as the horse is maintaining a firm and even contact with the bit, this position is easily maintained. It is easier for the horse if this forward position is adopted, as the rider's weight will be poised over the centre of gravity.

THE HANDS

It is essential for a rider to have good hands so let us consider what is meant by "Good Hands".

Through the reins, and therefore the hands, the rider has his fingers on, one might say, the pulse of the horse. He regulates the pace, directs the horse, and asks for "flexions" through this medium and it is of the utmost importance that he understands the influence he produces in this manner. The hands at all times must be light and responsive. They must be able to "give" and to "take" instantaneously, so much so that it becomes almost a reflex action.

Later it will be shown how a horse's training revolves round his mouth. In order to produce a well-balanced animal it is necessary for the horse to accept and hold the bit lightly in his mouth. He will then be ready at the slightest indication of the rider to obey any command given to him. None of this can be accomplished unless the rider has light and sensitive hands so that he is capable of feeling and correcting the slightest resistance on the part of the horse. If the horse resists in his mouth it is felt throughout his body, which becomes stiff and unyielding.

The rider does not use his hands alone; they must always work in conjunction with his back and legs, but it is the sense of touch through the fingers that makes or mars a horse's mouth, and the whole future of a rider's success in riding and training horses will depend upon whether his hands are sensitive to every reaction in the horse's mouth. He must know when and how they should "ask" and when they should be "soft". The hands should remain at the same level and be steady. Only one hand should "ask", while the other retains the light contact with the horse's mouth. When "asking" they must not be drawn back but used as in the "squeezing-of-a-sponge" and then remain soft and still again when the horse has "given" to the demanded flexion by relaxing his jaw. They must be ready to come into immediate action once again at the slightest sign of resistance from the horse.

The upper part of the rider's arms should hang loosely close to his sides. The forearms and wrists must be supple and relaxed so that they can act as a sort of buffer between the movement of the rider's body and the horse's mouth. As the rider becomes more efficient he will sit more erect and still, so the horse will feel no movement whatever when the hands are being polite and soft.

A very common fault seen in riding is too much movement of the hands. A horse's mouth is very sensitive and it is the rider's aim that it should remain so. But, if the hands are continually working backwards and forwards or up and down with every movement of his body, it is not surprising that the horse's mouth becomes insensitive, as he gets a repeated jab with every step he takes.

It will now be seen how important it is for the rider to have a strong and independent seat, because he must never use the reins in order to maintain his position in the saddle. The reins are only meant to guide and direct the movements of the horse and the rider must remember that the softer the hands the softer will be the horse, whilst heavy hands can only produce a heavy horse.

HOW TO HOLD THE REINS

The reins should normally be held in both hands. The following methods of holding the reins are recommended:

Single-rein bridle

(*i*) *Both reins in left hand.* The right rein should either be between the first and second fingers or between the first finger and thumb. The left rein should be outside the fourth finger. In the first method the slack of the rein should pass across the palm of the hand and between the first finger and thumb. In the second method the slack of the right rein passes across the palm of the hand and between the fourth finger and palm. The slack of the left rein passes across the palm of the hand and between the first finger and thumb.

(*ii*) *Reins in both hands.* First take the reins in the left hand as described above. Then place the right hand on the right rein with the rein held between the little and third fingers and take it from the left hand. The slack of the reins should pass between the finger and thumb of each hand. The hands should be held about four inches apart. The reins may be held outside the little finger if preferred.

Double-rein bridle

(*i*) *All four reins in left hand.* Place the little finger on the left hand between the two left reins and the second finger between the two right reins. The slack of the reins passes between the first finger and thumb.

(*ii*) *Reins in both hands.* The little finger of each hand should divide the reins.

The bridoon rein should be held on the outside.

Note. When the reins are held in one hand, either hand may be used.

PHYSICAL EXERCISES

The danger of injury to the rider by an accident or by excessive practice of these exercises, cannot be too strongly stressed. The horse must be sufficiently quiet for the exercise which is to be performed. In particular, the danger of strains and the adoption of false positions and grip, caused by performing exercises without stirrups, is emphasised. They should only be practised in short periods.

Rising from the saddle and resuming the seat

The position of the lower part of the leg should not change, the knees should not stiffen, and the rider should resume his seat slowly, without a bump. Particular care must be taken that the reins are not used to pull the rider up. This exercise can be done from the halt or the walk. The body should lean slightly forward from the waist as the seat is raised.

Turning round in the saddle to look behind

Without changing the position of the legs the rider should place one hand on the horse's neck, the other on the rear of the saddle, and turn from the waist, returning to the correct position; the exercise to be repeated to each side.

Turning the ankles

Having quitted the stirrups, turn the ankles both ways in a circular motion.

Arms swinging alternately from front to rear

The rider starts with both arms hanging straight down, then swings the arms, shoulder high, from front to rear with the right arm forward when the left arm is back. This exercise, as well as helping to develop the seat, creates energy and circulation. The head and body should be quite supple and move in rhythm.

Without stirrups, sitting down at the trot

This is a most beneficial exercise for developing a correct seat. Maintenance of a correct position is most important and care must be taken that there is no holding on by the reins or gripping with the back of the calf.

Touching the toes

The rider should hold the reins in the left hand and allow the right arm to hang down behind the thigh. No benefit will be derived from this exercise if the hand holding the reins is allowed to rest on the pony's neck. He should then reach down and touch the right toe with the fingers. The seat must remain well down in the saddle and the leg in the normal position. Having touched the toe the rider comes back quickly to the upright position. The exercise should be repeated several times with each hand. It can be done with or without stirrups. Particular care is needed that neither leg is drawn back, especially the one on the opposite side, nor the position of the knees altered.

Body bending backwards and forwards

Bend the body slightly forward from the waist, looking up between the horse's ears. Then bend slowly backwards until the shoulders are resting on the horse's quarters.

Note

The last two exercises are excellent for suppling the waist, but in order to avoid possible injury to the rider, care must be taken to see that the beginner's mount is quiet.

At first the rider will find it uncomfortable to keep the knee and thigh continually on the saddle. This is due to the prominent muscle on the inside of the thigh. This will be more pronounced in the case of people with short round thighs than those with the long flat variety. In the early stages this muscle should be pulled round behind and the thigh laid on to the saddle. The difference will at once be noticed and the grip will appear to have become stronger, without any extra effort.

THE AIDS

The word "Aids" has two meanings.

    (1) The signals by means of which the rider conveys his intentions to the horse, signals which the horse must be taught to understand and obey.

    (2) The means at our disposal for producing these signals.

For example, when a young horse is being lunged, the trainer's means for producing the necessary signals will be the cavesson, the whip and the voice, while the signals by which he conveys his intentions will be the action of the cavesson, whip and voice. By the intelligent application of these aids used in conjunction, and by instantly rewarding obedience, the trainer will teach the horse to answer to the correct aid.

The means at our disposal can be subdivided into Natural and Artificial aids.

(1) Natural: The hands, legs, body and voice.

(2) Artificial: Whips, spurs, martingales, etc.

NATURAL AIDS

The body

The body, through the back muscles and their influence on the seat, plays an important part in riding. The back muscles influence the seat in two ways; when relaxed they enable the rider to maintain his balance under adverse conditions and so lend security to the seat; when braced—i.e. when the spine is straightened—they influence the horse in accordance with the corresponding hand and leg aids.

The seat

It is only from the basis of a firm, deep seat that the rider is able to gain the correct use of his legs. It is through the seat that the rider will first perceive the horse's evasions that emanate, as many do, from the hindquarters.

Note. Throughout this book the words "straighten the spine" have been used to replace the phrase "brace the back". The intended meaning is identical.

The legs

(1) Create impulsion or energy.

(2) Guide and control the hindquarters.

To increase pace or energy the inside of the calves of the legs are applied against the horse's sides, repeating the pressure as necessary. The legs should not be drawn far back nor should the toes be turned out too much.

To guide and control the hindquarters the rider may use either leg independently in the manner described above, except that the leg is drawn slightly back to indicate the way in which it is desired to move or control the hindquarters.

The hands, by means of the reins:

    (1) Regulate the energy created by the legs.

    (2) Control the forehand.

    (3) Guide, check or allow pace.

The voice

Assists in controlling the horse in the early stages of training. The voice can encourage or soothe, check or frighten.

The aids should work in harmony with one another.

ARTIFICIAL AIDS

Whips, spurs and martingales, all come under the heading of "Artificial Aids".

They are supplementary aids to the legs and hands and a means of correction.

The stick

The best form of stick is usually made of cane and should be between 24 and 26 inches long. It is carried loosely in the palm of the hand with 4 to 6 inches protruding in front of the hand. If it is carried correctly it will be pointing towards the horse's opposite ear.

Should the horse not respond to the rider's legs the stick may be used to reinforce the leg aids so that the horse will learn to obey the seat and leg aids alone. It can be used in either hand just behind the rider's leg; the hand holding the stick must be removed from the reins when the stick is used. As soon as the horse obeys the stick should be put back in the correct position. The application of the stick by a flick of the wrist with the hand still holding a rein, except by an expert, upsets the proper contact with the horse's mouth and should not be done.

To hit a horse properly, as opposed to using a flick of the wrist, the stick should be held in the hand with the butt by the little finger and the long end between the thumb and first finger.

To put the reins into one hand and change the grip so that the stick is held as above is a knack which has to be learnt and needs practice.

It is important that the rider should be able to use the whip in either hand, the left being more useful than the right. Inexpert horsemen are apt always to use the right hand; the horse quickly realises this and generally runs out to the left when refusing a fence.

The stick may be used for punishment in rare cases when a horse refuses to obey. It will then be applied behind the leg, definitely and without delay. The rider must be satisfied that his horse is not frightened or puzzled but understands quite clearly what is wanted; that the horse is not lame or unwell nor full of gaiety and merely pulling the rider's leg. Above all the rider's temper must be under control and he must not be frightened. On the rare occasions when punishment is merited it must be given immediately, with calm and cool deliberation and must not be excessive.

A horse should never be hit over the head; serious injuries may result if this is done.

The cutting whip

A cutting whip can be of various lengths. Under F.E.I. and B.S.J.A. rules this is limited to 30 inches. An extra long one is useful for schooling or polo. A shorter variety is used for racing. Broad pieces of leather bound on to the end of the whip make a considerable noise when the horse is hit and prevent cutting or marking.

The use of the whip when racing, in the hands of the expert, is not dealt with in this book.

The hunting whip

The hunting whip should never be carried without the thong and lash. The lash is a small piece of silk or whipcord at the end of the thong. The hunting whip should be held at the point of balance and carried in the same way as the stick, with the hook to the rear, pointing downwards.

Spurs

The object of the spurs is to make the horse light and responsive to the leg. They should only be used by riders who are sufficiently advanced to have complete control of their legs. They should only be applied if the horse does not respond to the pressure of the leg. Spurs with rowels should never be used. Spurs with curved necks should point downwards; they must not be worn upside down.

Care should be taken to have spur straps cut the right length so that the spur lies horizontal along the seam of the riding boot.

The spur is applied gently, with the inside of the spur against the horse's side, care being taken not to turn the toe out so that the back of the spur is used.

Martingales

(1) **Standing Martingale.** A strap attached at one end to the noseband, and at the other between the horse's forelegs to the girth, supported by a neck strap. It should be used for no other purpose than to prevent the horse carrying its head above the angle of control, and not in order to hold the head down. It should never be attached to a dropped noseband.

Fitting

When the horse's head is up in the correct position for moving, and the martingale is attached at both ends, put your hand underneath the martingale and push it up; it should just reach into the horse's gullet.

(2) **Running Martingale.** One end is attached between the horse's forelegs to the girth and the other end divides into two straps, each with a ring at the end, through which the reins are passed. The martingale is supported by a neck strap. If used on the curb rein, care must be taken that the rings of the martingale are not so large as to constitute a danger by getting over the rings on the bit. The running martingale is an artificial aid to prevent the horse carrying his head above the angle of control.

Fitting

When attached to the girth with both rings up one side, these rings should reach to the withers.

The neck strap for both standing and running martingales should fit so that it will admit the width of the hand at the withers. The buckle should be on the near side of the neck.

(3) **The Irish Martingale** consists of two rings connected by a strap 4 to 6 inches long. The snaffle reins are passed through the rings, beneath the horse's neck. It is used to keep the reins in place and prevent them from going over the horse's head.

APPLICATION OF THE AIDS

This requires a knowledge of techniques as well as natural ability.

In every case the lightest possible aid should be applied to get the best possible results. The application of the aids on a young horse must be clear, definite and even exaggerated. As the training proceeds, the aids will become more delicate until, with the trained horse, they become practically invisible to the onlooker whilst at the same time maintaining their clarity to the horse.

Every aid requires the complete harmony of body, legs and hands, without which it is quite impossible to get smooth results, and the aids must be sustained to the necessary degree throughout all movements. By placing the horse in the correct position before the aid is given, he can obey more easily what the aid indicates (Place before you propel).

To increase pace to walk or trot

Close both legs, straighten the spine and ease the reins, still maintaining a light contact with the horse's mouth. As soon as the horse obeys, the pressure of the legs should be sufficient only to maintain the desired pace and energy.

The extended trot

Increase the pressure of both legs, asking the horse to lengthen his stride but not to quicken it. It is most important to keep the rhythm and to maintain the contact with the horse's mouth. The horse should not increase the weight on the reins but his neck should be lengthened. This should not be attempted in the early stages of training.

To decrease pace or halt

Close both legs, straighten the spine and bring the horse up into a still hand. He should decrease pace smoothly, with a steady head-carriage and, when halting, should stand squarely on all four legs. As soon as the horse has obeyed, relax the pressure of the legs and the feeling on the reins, then maintain the pace as desired.

The right turn on the forehand (from the halt only)

Maintain a feeling on both reins to prevent the horse moving forward, the horse's head bent very slightly to the right. With the weight of the rider's body central, the right leg is applied distinctly behind the girth, in order to move the quarters to the left. The left leg remains close to the girth and the horse's side ready to prevent him from moving backwards. The pivoting leg is the off-fore. The right hind-leg should cross in front of the left hind-leg. As soon as the horse has taken the required number of steps, he should be asked to move forward without pausing.

The left turn on the forehand (from the halt only)

Reverse the above.

Right turn on the haunches (Half Pirouette)

To turn to the right the rider leads the forehand round with the right rein supported by the left; the left leg, acting behind the girth, prevents the quarters going to the left while the right leg, at the girth, maintains impulsion and keeps the horse from stepping back. The left foreleg should cross in front of the right foreleg while the right hind leg marks time, maintaining the walking pace.

The horse should maintain his impulsion; he must not move backwards or sideways.

Left turn on the haunches (Half Pirouette)

Reverse the above.

The rein-back

Before commencing a rein-back, the horse must be standing to attention with a fairly low head carriage and a relaxed jaw.

Apply both legs and seat in order to send the horse up into the bit, but instead of yielding with the hands as in the case of the walk, retain the pressure. When the horse has taken the required number of steps backwards, the rider must ease the reins to allow the horse to halt or to go forward as required. The horse should rein-back in a straight line in two-time, moving alternate diagonals, with the head carried correctly. If the rider has to pull at the horse's mouth to obtain the rein-back, the horse is not ready for this movement.

To circle or turn to the right

Throughout the movement keep the seat in the centre and lowest part of the saddle, the rider sitting square to the movement of the horse, the head erect and the eyes looking forward over the horse's ears. Guide the forehand round to the right with the inside rein, which is responsible for bend and direction; the outside rein, which controls balance and pace, must allow the necessary movement of the horse's head to the right without checking. The rider's right (inner) leg, applied at the girth, maintains impulsion while the left (outer) leg, being farther back controls the hindquarters, ensuring that the hind feet follow in the tracks of the forefeet.

The horse's head must not be turned outwards nor should he bend his head and neck inwards more than the rest of his body.

In the elementary stages a more "open" rein should be used with the horse's head slightly bent in the direction in which he is going and the hind feet following in the tracks of the forefeet.

Aids for the canter on a named leg

To canter off-fore leading (*right canter*). With the right rein bend the horse slightly to the right, sit well down in the saddle and, with the pressure of both legs, the left further back than the right, make the horse strike off into a canter. The left leg should be applied distinctly behind the girth to prevent the horse's quarters swinging out; the right leg at the girth to increase the impulsion.

With an untrained horse the canter should only be attempted from a trot while circling.

The rider must on no account look down to see which leg is leading; he must learn to feel which shoulder is slightly in advance of the other and which hind leg comes to the ground first.

To canter near-fore leading (*left canter*). Reverse the above.

Terms at the canter

A horse should always canter "united".

A horse is said to be cantering "true" or "united" when the leading foreleg and the leading hind leg appear to be on the same side and is said to be cantering "disunited" when the leading hind leg appears to be on the opposite side to the leading foreleg.

A horse is said to be cantering "false" and "counter-lead" when he is cantering to the left with the off-fore leading, or to the right with the near-fore leading.

*BITTING

PRINCIPLES OF BITTING

For the man who knows the principles of horse training and is possessed of a firm seat and good hands, the theory of bitting is a small subject. But the man who tries to find some mechanical contrivance to put in a horse's mouth will seldom achieve permanent satisfactory results.

It must be remembered that the power to control a horse by a bit is only accomplished by the system of correction and reward. If the horse obeys the action of the reins, the rider should give to him at once.

The whole principle of bitting, etc., is the application of pressure on the mouth, the horse giving way to it by relaxing the jaw, and the instantaneous acknowledgement by the hands of the rider.

A horse may pull for any or all of the following reasons:

(1) Excitability.

(2) Lack of balance and training.

(3) Pain or fear of the bit.

(4) A hard mouth.

Excitability

The majority of young horses will be excitable when first ridden in company or introduced to hounds. They will reach at their bridles, throw their heads about and, if allowed to, attempt to run away. At this stage great care must be taken not to damage their mouths. They must not be allowed to "go on", but must be taken away from the crowd directly should they show signs of losing their mouths. They should be ridden in a snaffle and their lips should be watched constantly for cuts and bruises.

---

*NOTE: This subject is also covered by the Pony Club film strip book, "Bits and Bitting".

Lack of balance and training

Before his muscles are developed and he has accustomed himself to the weight of the rider, a horse will often, through lack of balance, experience difficulty in reducing his pace. It should be realised that at this stage the horse's mouth is still unmade and so unless the rider uses tact and sympathy in reducing the pace, much harm will result. What may be mistaken for a hard mouth (when it is really only the horse's inability to respond quickly) may easily be made one by the rider using force.

Pain or fear of the bit

A badly-fitting bit or a sore mouth will often cause a horse to pull in order to get away from the pain.

A dry mouth, swallowed tongue and tongue over the bit are all evasions from pain caused by bitting.

A dry mouth is the result of the tongue being drawn back and the mouth being slightly open. The air passes rapidly through the mouth and quickly dries it up. In their dry state the bars of the mouth are easily torn and bruised. A dry mouth is usually associated with an "unmade" mouth and a stiff jaw.

A swallowed tongue and tongue over the bit are caused by the horse trying to evade the pressure of the bit. In either case the bars are easily damaged and if the tongue is over the bit, the under part of the tongue becomes torn.

The conformation of a horse's head and neck is of considerable importance in bitting. If the channel which lies between the branches of the lower jaw is too narrow, or the head and neck are too closely coupled, the animal will have difficulty in flexing correctly. A horse with either fault is usually unpleasant to ride, and if the rider persists in trying to obtain the correct head-carriage, pain will be caused and the horse, as a result, will become a puller. It is better, in such cases, to allow the horse to find his own natural head carriage.

A hard mouth

The bit other than a snaffle lies on the tongue and on the bars of the mouth which are extremely sensitive. They are thinly covered with skin, in which there is a mass of nerves. When once these nerves are destroyed, feeling will disappear and the animal will become hard mouthed.

The nerves in the bars of the mouth are destroyed by continual bit injuries and bruising due to pulling at young, undeveloped and excitable animals, to severe and badly-fitting bits, or to the horse having a stiff jaw and not accepting the bit.

It is a mistake to increase the severity of the bit on an excitable or pulling horse. He should be put back in a snaffle and taught to relax his jaw, as described on page 59.

BITS AND THEIR USES

There are three bits, the snaffle, the double bridle and the pelham, though there are many varieties of each.

The Snaffle

The jointed snaffle acts on the outside of the bars of the mouth, the lips, or the corners of the mouth, according to the hand action.

The use of the snaffle, in conjunction with the rider's legs, is to teach the horse to accept the bit with a still and correct head-carriage and supple jaw.

The following are some of the different kinds of snaffles:

(1) *The smooth, jointed snaffle,* made of metal with a joint in the middle, is the one chiefly in use and, if fairly thick, it is the best kind to use.

(2) The egg-butt snaffle which is less likely to pinch or damage the horse's lips than the ordinary ring snaffle.

(3) The snaffle with cheeks (see figure 3) and a thick jointed mouthpiece. The cheeks prevent the bit from rubbing the sides of the horse's mouth or from being pulled through the mouth from one side to the other. The keeper, holding the cheek to the bridle, prevents the bit from turning over in the mouth.

(4) *The half-moon and straight-bar unjointed snaffle,* made of vulcanite, rubber or metal. These are very mild and can be used on horses whose mouths have been injured.

(5) *The twisted snaffle.* This is severe and should be avoided.

(6) *The gag snaffle.* The action of this bit is on the corners of the lips. It is very powerful and should only be used by experts.

(7) *The snaffle and dropped noseband.* The dropped noseband should only be used in conjunction with a snaffle. It should be carefully fitted so that the front strap is well above the nostrils, where it cannot restrict the horse's breathing. The back strap passes below the mouthpiece of the bit and is adjusted so as to prevent the horse from crossing his jaw or opening his mouth wide. A dropped noseband also helps to prevent him from getting his tongue over the bit and helps to keep his mouth moist by preventing him from opening his mouth and drawing back his tongue.

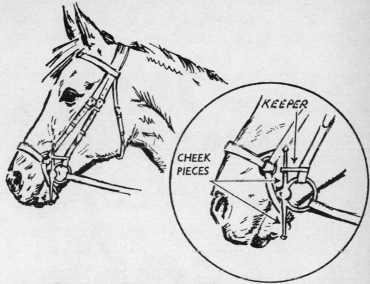

FIGURE 3.   SNAFFLE BRIDLE AND DROPPED NOSEBAND

The Double Bridle

This consists of a bridoon, which is a snaffle with a thinner mouthpiece than those described above, a curb-bit with a fixed or movable mouthpiece and a curb chain with a lip strap.

It should only be used when the horse has been taught, in a snaffle bridle, to offer no resistance in his mouth, to go forward freely and to come back to the rider with a relaxed jaw. Then the curb-bit will afford additional control to the rider and help to give a lighter aid.

Its function is:

(a) The bridoon acts in the same way as a jointed snaffle.

(b) The curb can act at the same time as the bridoon to give
a more refined and imperceptible aid and to help to maintain a relaxed jaw.

FIGURE 4.   THE DOUBLE BRIDLE

EQUITATION
29

Bits permitted in F.E.I. and B.H.S. Contests

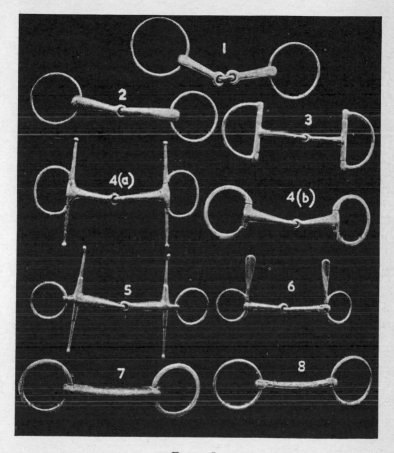

FIGURE 5.

Plate 1.
  (1) Ordinary snaffle with double-jointed mouthpiece.
  (2) Ordinary snaffle with joined mouthpiece.
  (3) Racing snaffle.
  (4) Egg-butt snaffle (a) with cheeks: (b) without cheeks.
  (5) Other type of snaffle with cheeks.
  (6) Snaffle with upper cheeks only.
  (7) Rubber snaffle, unjointed.
  (8) Unjointed snaffle.

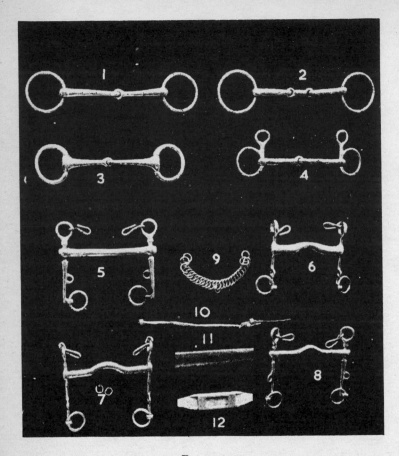

FIGURE 6.

Plate 2.
Various Bridoon bits
(1) Ordinary bridoon bit.
(2) Bridoon bit with two joints.
(3) Egg-butt bridoon bit.
(4) Bridoon bit with cheeks.
Various types of curb bits
(5) Half-moon curb bit.
(6) Curb bit with curved cheeks and port.

(7) Curb bit with loops for the lipstrap on the cheeks and with port.
(8) Curb bit with port and sliding mouthpiece (Weymouth).
(9) Curb chain.
(10) Lipstrap.
(11) Rubber cover for curb chain.
(12) Leather cover for curb chain.

Fitting

The bridoon should lie in the horse's mouth as high as possible without causing the lips to wrinkle. The curb bit should be immediately below it. The curb chain, which should be thick and flat, should lie snugly in the chin groove and be sufficiently tight to allow the cheek pieces of the bit to be drawn back to an angle of 45 degrees with the horse's mouth. If too loose, the curb chain is inclined to ride up above the chin groove when in use, or, when not in use, to flap about and irritate the horse. The lip strap should pass through the ring which hangs from the bottom of the curb chain and be fitted loosely.

Action of the curb bit

The mouth-piece presses on the bars and the tongue. The cheeks of the bit act as a lever to increase the pressure on the bars of the mouth. The curb rein must therefore be used with great delicacy. The curb chain is the fulcrum and should be painless.

When the curb bit is used without a bridoon, the constant pressure on the lower jaw is inclined to numb the horse's mouth and kill all feeling; it is therefore not advocated.

The Pelham

This bit is a combination of the curb and bridoon on one mouth-piece, to the cheek of which is attached the bridoon and curb reins, thus trying to make the one bit perform the duties of two. This, in principle, is not a sound policy, but the fact remains that some horses will go better in a pelham than they will in anything else.

Sometimes with a pelham a single rein is used, attached to a leather rounding itself attached to the bridoon and curb rings on the cheek of the bit. This cannot be advocated for use by those who wish to take advantage of the correct action of either bit, but it has proved advantageous in some cases.

BALANCE AND COLLECTION

In dealing with balance and collection, it must be remembered that a horse's forefeet, when on the ground, cannot be in front of a perpendicular line drawn through the nose. Thus, as the length of a horse's stride is increased, the head and neck must be extended.

Balance comes before collection. Unless a horse is balanced he cannot be collected.

Balance

A horse is said to be balanced when his own weight and that of his rider are distributed in such a way as to allow him to use himself with maximum ease and efficiency. The head and neck form the governing factors, or balancing pole, in weight distribution. It is by their position that a horse carries his centre of gravity forward or backward as the paces are extended or collected. A young horse, when at liberty, naturally learns to balance himself. When he is mounted, this balance will be upset by the weight of the rider and the centre of balance is displaced. Balance is acquired by developing the muscles, especially of the back and hind legs, by means of physical exercises. These include increasing and decreasing pace, both on the level and up and down hills and slopes, starting and stopping, turning, circling and jumping. In fact, balance improves as training progresses. The rider should not attempt to achieve it by artificially raising the horse's head.

When in progression, the centre of balance will constantly be displaced in one direction or another. As the pace increases the displacement will become further and further forward. One of the advantages of a short stirrup for the jockey is that he can more easily put his weight forward over the centre of balance.

Collection

Collection is the concentration of the horse's energy, when the whole of his body is collected into a shortened form with a relaxed jaw, on a very light rein, with even more active hind-legs, so that he has the maximum control over his limbs and is in a position to obey instantly the slightest indication of his rider.

To achieve this, the horse's muscles must undergo intensive training, in order to be capable of standing the extra strain put on to the hindquarters. True collection can never be obtained from the front by pulling back with the hands. By so doing, the rider will restrict the fluid and supple movements of the horse. The propelling force must come from behind and the impulsion so generated be controlled by the hands.

JUMPING

THE HORSE

Before discussing the rider, it is necessary to study the horse in the approach, the take-off, the period of suspension and the landing.

The approach

The horse lowers his head and neck and stretches the neck. This allows him to balance himself and prepare to make his jump.

The take-off

At this moment the horse shortens his neck, slightly raises his head and lifts up his forehand. He brings his hocks under him, stretches his head and neck and makes his spring upward and forward.

Period of suspension

Now the head and neck are stretched to full extent and downwards. The hind legs, having left the ground, are gathered up under the belly.

Landing

As the horse is landing, his head comes up and his neck shortens.

THE RIDER

The Jumping Position is the position that can be adopted and maintained at all paces and throughout all stages of the jump. In circumstances such as a horse showing disobedience, the normal riding position can easily be resumed.

The jumping position

The rider's head up, looking in the direction in which he is going; the body as still as possible; the back straight and supple, with the shoulders forward and the weight taken on the knee and thigh pressing down into the heel; the seat bones close to, but not pressing down into the saddle; the stirrup leathers at such a length that the rider can easily maintain his position, while keeping in balance with the movements of the horse. The rider must avoid any tendency to stand up in the stirrups by straightening the knee.

The arms slightly bent at the elbow (which should not be allowed to be thrust out sideways), forming a straight line from the elbow, through the forearms, hands and reins, to the horse's mouth. The shoulders, arms and fingers should be supple, so that they can follow the movement of the horse's head, while maintaining contact without any interference.

Length of stirrup and position of legs

The rider will require a shorter length for hunting than for dressage (training) and still shorter for show jumping or racing. The feet must be sufficiently engaged in the stirrups to avoid losing them; the heels lower than the toes to allow the flexibility of the ankles to play their part as shock absorbers. The lower part of the legs remains close to the sides of the horse, with the stirrup leathers vertical.

The approach, over the jump and landing

In the early stages of jumping when the rider should be on a horse that will jump small fences without hesitation he will approach the obstacle in the jumping position with a rhythmic stride.

As the horse rises at the jump the rider should have the feeling of being close to the saddle; he should maintain the jumping position throughout by keeping in balance and following the movement of the horse; he must avoid allowing his weight to slip back on the horse's loins; he should allow his hands and arms to follow the movement of the horse's head and neck giving him full freedom whilst still retaining contact with the mouth. In this manner the beginner will gain confidence in jumping and find his balance and rhythm.

Since he will not always be able to present his horse in rhythm he must cultivate the suppleness of waist needed to negotiate an awkward fence or to respond to an awkward take-off.

More advanced jumping

In more advanced jumping, the rider can assist the horse to arrive right at the obstacle. He can regulate the impulsion and length of stride before the jump, but he must always approach the fence with increasing impulsion. Pace must not be mistaken for impulsion.

1   2

FIGURE 7.   THE JUMPING POSITION

It is the art of arriving "right" at the obstacle which makes the good and safe jumper, and this can only be achieved by practice and dressage. The larger the fence, the more accurate must be the approach. Any correction should be made at least three strides away from the obstacle so that the horse is not interfered with in those last strides, but is able to concentrate on the jump and make his own adjustments.

In this stage the rider should learn to ride the approach with his seat bones in light contact with the saddle and his shoulders a trifle less forward.

Only in this position has the rider his full powers to carry out the delicate operation of lengthening or shortening the stride whilst retaining balance and the required impulsion in the horse and only in this position will he feel instantaneously a resistance in the horse which, unless immediately corrected, might lead to refusal or run-out.

The rider will regain the Jumping position in the rhythm of the take-off.

3   4

In practice the rider may approach the fence in the Jumping position when he is sure of his horse and the fence is straightforward but if he has any doubt about either he should ride the approach with his seat bones in light contact with the saddle.

Advantages of the jumping position

The jumping position, while accepting the classical principles of riding, allows the rider to follow the movements of the horse and, at the same time, to employ the supple thigh, knee and ankle joints as shock absorbers. It is therefore used when negotiating steep hills, ramps, etc. The rider should practice the position on the flat at the trot and canter and also over cavalletti and jumping grids.

JUMPING AT HOME

This is fun and very good for rider and horse provided it is carried out wisely. A horse jumps well when he approaches the fence with confidence and at an even pace as directed by the rider, takes off at such a distance from the fence as to make the least possible effort necessary to clear the jump, jumps with a supple neck and spine and lands quietly to continue at the desired pace.

A horse jumps badly when he approaches the fence nervously, refuses, runs out or props at the take-off and bucks over, or rushes into the fence with his head in the air and is over-excited.

Bad jumping may be attributed either to bad schooling or bad riding.

It is a mistake to go on jumping for too long especially on hard ground. The horse may get sore and bored. If he has jumped well stop jumping and make much of him.

CONSTRUCTION OF SCHOOLING FENCES

For ordinary every-day jumping it should be the aim of the rider to improve the style of the horse's jumping and to increase his confidence. The rider will also be trying to improve his own ability to ride over fences. Much therefore depends on the construction of schooling fences.

The following points should be considered:

(1) There should be a wide variety of fences which may include poles, bush fences, walls, tree trunks, banks, ditches, water, etc.—fences which are upright, others which involve a spread; fences which can be seen through and fences which cannot; doubles.

(2) Fences should be sited where the going is as good as possible at all times of the year. Steps can be taken to improve the ground by adding cinders, by drainage and by "treading in" when the ground is cut up.

(3) It is very tiresome and frequently a disadvantage from a schooling point of view to have to dismount to put up the jump whenever the horse hits it. Solid fences, which may be smaller, are therefore best. The thicker the poles the better—and therefore more safely—the horse jumps.

It is possible to make solid fences adjustable by the means suggested in "Training the Young Horse and Pony" under Loose Jumping.

(4) A horse will jump more freely going towards home or other horses. If he rushes, jump him the opposite way.

(5) A horse judges his distance from a jump looking at the part of the fence on or nearest to the ground—the "ground-line". It is therefore easier for him—and the rider—if there is a distinct ground-line.

(6) Faggots, pea-sticks, branches or even a pole placed on the ground make a distinct ground-line nearer to the horse than the top of the fence.

(7) The correct place for a horse to take off—depending on the fence and the speed of the horse—in order to jump most easily will be approximately the same distance from the top of the fence as the height of the fence—or 50 per cent more—i.e. from 4 to 6 feet in front of a 4 foot fence.

(8) Practice jumps should not exceed 2 ft. 6 in. to 3 ft. in height. 2 ft. is generally big enough for ponies.

(9) It is better to increase the spread rather than the height of the jump in order to obtain further effort.

(10) To increase the spread place another pole at the same height on movable supports on the landing side.

(11) To increase the height, if poles are not adjustable, put another pole on movable supports above the fixed pole.

(12) Parallel poles cause the horse to look into the fence and so stretch the neck in good style.

(13) Cavalletti or poles placed on the ground in front of the fence cause the horse to look down and steady himself. They can, by being placed at suitable distances, guide the

horse to the correct take-off position. The correct distance between a "guide" cavalletti and the fence, if one canter stride is required, will vary according to the stride of the horse and must be decided by experiment. An approximate measurement is 22 feet.

FIGURE 8.　EXAMPLE OF A PRACTICE FENCE

(14) Jumping fences in a continuous straight line tends to excite horses. Jumping fences on a circle helps to quieten them down as well as encouraging them to lower their heads, bend their backs and become more supple.

(15) To increase the difficulty, for example, of an experienced horse that must learn to jump awkward fences out hunting or on cross-country courses, remove the ground-line altogether.

(16) It is essential to include ditches amongst the schooling fences and to have water in some of them. It is necessary to teach all horses to face open water at an early stage. A series of small ditches increasing in size is very valuable; if they are made with a sloping bottom and lined with cement they will not fall in and the rain is generally sufficient to keep them filled.

RIDING OVER PRACTICE JUMPS

(1) The main object of riding over practice jumps is to improve the performance of the rider and of the horse. Both should enjoy themselves.

(2) There should be as good a selection as possible of fences with a wide variety, both natural and artificial. The construction of fences has already been described. Some of them should be sited on slopes and they should be jumped both up and down hill.

(3) The rider will not be able to ride his best over fences unless he has a good saddle which fits him and the horse, in which he can sit securely in the lowest part and which is cut sufficiently forward to allow him to keep his knee on the saddle. He will normally use a plain snaffle; a curb bit should not be used when schooling but a martingale strap or stirrup leather around the horse's neck is almost essential for use in an emergency.

(4) Neither the rider nor the horse should be "overfaced" and only fences within the capacity of both should be attempted. A start should be made with cavalletti followed by small, solid fences. Tree trunks and telegraph poles are excellent.

(5) Although keenness is to be encouraged the horse should not be over-excited. If he is, steps must be taken, by means of quiet circling at slow paces and cavalletti, to calm him. The horse must be obedient and under control and must not be allowed to hot up and rush either before or after jumping.

(6) The rider must ride as well as he can and avoid at all costs jobbing the horse in the mouth or being "left behind". If he is he must allow the reins to slip through his fingers and hold on to the martingale strap.

(7) Jumping must be practised at all paces. After a start walking over poles or ditches work should continue at a trot and when under control at this pace the horse can be jumped at a canter. Similarly the larger fences should not be attempted until both rider and horse are performing satisfactorily over cavalletti and the small fences.

(8) Do not sicken the horse by jumping the same fence over and over again without variation.

(9) If a horse is obedient, well trained and has not been overfaced he should jump whatever he is told to and should never refuse. If he does and the fence is not too large or will knock down it is sometimes better to push him on over the fence than to turn back and have another go.

In the case of a run-out the horse should always be turned back against the direction in which he has run out—i.e. if he went to the left he must be turned back to the right and the approach made at a slight angle from the left.

In the case of either refusal or run-out it is generally wise to re-present the horse with a short approach.

(10) The practice should always finish with a good jump, however small. The horse which has done well should immediately be rewarded by a good, sound pat on the neck. Finally reward a good school by dismounting, slackening the girth and then giving the horse a tit-bit, allowing him to graze and walk quietly home.

CAVALLETTI

Six or even four cavalletti are a very useful possession. They serve a variety of purposes in the schooling of horses and riders, and they can be used to build up many different types of jumps, e.g. a "Grid", "Parallel Bars", "In and Out", "Oxer", "Triple", "Jump with Wings".

One cavalletti can be placed so as to fix the pole at 10 ins., 15 ins. or 19 ins. Extra height and spread can be obtained by building up one on top of the other. Figure 9 shows a useful method of constructing cavalletti.

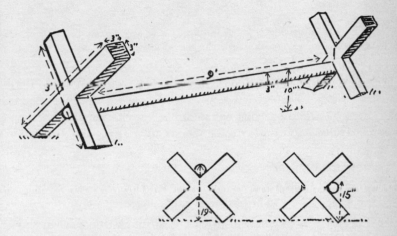

FIGURE 9. CONSTRUCTIONAL DIAGRAM OF CAVALLETTI

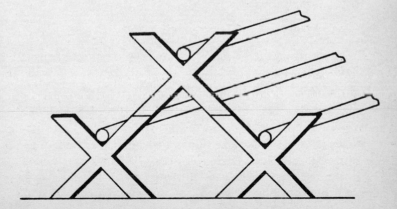

Horses may be introduced to the idea of cavalletti by using thick poles lying on the ground. They are less likely to be kicked about if they are square or, if round, have a piece of board nailed on at each end to prevent them rolling. They are used in the same way as cavalletti but at slightly closer distances.

The use of cavalletti for schooling has many advantages:

Value for the Rider

(1) Gradually develops the correct position over jumps, combining balance, suppleness, style and strength.

(2) Gives the feeling of rhythm and the ability to judge the horse's stride.

Value for the Horse

(1) A physical exercise which develops muscles, balance, suppleness, agility, stamina and obedience.

(2) Develops ease and rhythm of stride, with impulsion and engagement of the hindquarters.

(3) Develops calmness and the correct technique in jumping.

Method of Use

Every horse needs to be introduced to cavalletti poles gradually so that he will always approach and negotiate them calmly with a supple back and loin and a stretched and lowered neck.

The following exercises are easier if there is a dismounted assistant to handle and replace the poles.

Stage 1. At a walk. The purpose is simply to introduce the horse to the cavalletti. Begin with plain poles on the ground. Later the exercise may be continued with cavalletti, introducing one at a time at the lowest height.

Start with one pole and progress by introducing more equally spaced approximately 4 to 5 feet apart. When the horse will walk calmly increase the pace to a trot for the last few strides.

Stage 2. At a trot. The poles, or cavalletti at the lowest height, beginning with one, should be placed, as before, from 4 to 5 feet apart according to the horse's stride. In some cases, with a long striding horse, they may even be as much as 6 ft. apart. Introduce more poles gradually until the horse can negotiate six in a row with lightness and regular rhythm. (See figure 10 left side).

Horses which rush their fences may be started over poles placed six or seven yards apart crossing only one at a time and circling, several times if necessary, after each pole. Only when they will walk calmly, with a regular hoof beat over one, should they be allowed to continue over the next and only when they will walk correctly down the line of poles should trotting be attempted.

Stage 3. Introduce a small jump at the end of the line of six cavalletti by removing pole No. 5 and placing it up against pole No. 6 (See figure 10, right side).

The jump can be gradually widened and raised in height (see figure 9), and its precise distance from the last trotting cavalletti shortened or lengthened, according to the results required.

Stage 4. Introduce two jumps into the line of cavalletti at approximately 9 ft. distances, by removing pole No. 3 and placing it up against pole No. 4.

Stage 5. Introduce three jumps. The time taken to reach Stage 5 is unpredictable, but it is essential to "progress slowly" in order to maintain calmness and a correct physical development during all lessons.

The last jump can be of various designs, in order to introduce the young horse to different kinds of fences (see example in figure 8).

Note. For trotting strides, the height of the cavalletti should not exceed 10 ins., or the horse will be obliged to "hop" to negotiate them.

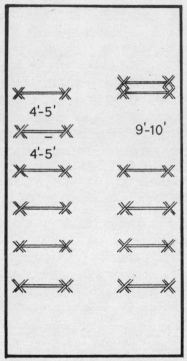

FIGURE 10.   POLES OR CAVALLETTI PLACED FOR TROTTING

Stage 6. At a canter. Begin with one cavalletti, at the middle height. Progress by introducing more, as in Stage 2, approximately 18 to 20 ft. apart. A keen horse will often jump two at once if there are several close together. Then insert others between these at 9 to 10 ft. distances (see figure 11, left side) until the horse is able to negotiate a line of poles at a canter 9 to 10 ft. apart.

The last jump may be built up, as before, and the cavalletti
turned to their maximum height.

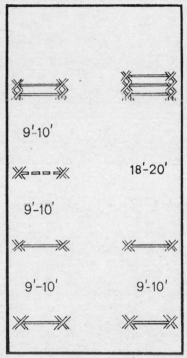

FIGURE 11.   CAVALLETTI PLACED FOR CANTERING

A cavalletti may be used as a "distance guide" before a built-up
fence, to help the horse to arrive at the right place for the take-off
(see figure 11, right side). The distance the pole is placed away
from the jump will vary according to the horse's length of stride,
but approximately 18 to 20 ft. may be found most suitable.

A "Box" of Cavalletti (See figure 12)

This is a useful variation to placing the cavalletti in a straight line and is excellent for developing obedience and agility. The cavalletti are placed at right-angles to one another to form a "box",

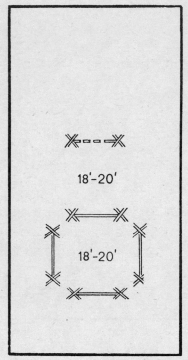

FIGURE 12.   A "BOX" OF CAVELLETTI

with spaces at the corners, through which the horse may pass without jumping. They may be placed to allow for one or two strides, e.g. approximately 18 ft. or approximately 27 ft.

The horse, or the ride, may be circled round the jumps, or ridden normally round the manege, and individually called in to pass through the gaps, to jump in and out, or to pass through a gap, then jump, etc., etc. The jumps may be built-up and varied as desired.

Single Cavalletti may be spread about the field or school, numbered or plain, as doubles or parallel poles and jumped in named or any order. This is another good exercise for horses which rush their fences.

COMMON CAUSES OF BAD JUMPING AND REFUSALS

(1) Lack of training.

(2) The horse being asked to jump fences that are too big or difficult for the stage of training.

(3) Falls and subsequent lack of nerve.

(4) Weakness and lack of condition.

(5) The horse being sore from splint, tendon, foot, etc.

(6) Badly fitted and uncomfortable saddle or bridle.

(7) Memories of pain caused by a jab in the mouth, etc.

(8) The rider over-shortening the stride during the approach.

(9) Bad presentation of the horse to the fence and lack of determination by the rider.

The cure for any of the above is first to diagnose correctly the cause, and then to use common sense to counteract it.

(7), (8) and (9) are clear indications that the rider is not good enough to school a young horse. The training must either be undertaken by somebody else, or the rider must set out to improve his riding under the supervision of an instructor. When he starts schooling again, he should follow the procedure outlined for (2) below, for a horse which has been overfaced.

(4), (5) and (6) are matters of stable management.

In the case of (4), weakness and lack of condition, it would be well to take the advice of the veterinary surgeon or an experienced stud groom. Probably the first points needing attention will be to

FIGURE 13.   AN UNCOMFORTABLE BRIDLE WILL CAUSE BAD JUMPING

file the teeth, and to dose for worms. Then follow the advice given in this Manual under "Health, Condition and Exercise".

For (5), lameness, get the blacksmith to examine the foot and call in the vet.

If the fault lies in a badly fitting saddle or bridle (6), it should obviously be correctly fitted and adjusted if possible. But it may be that the bridle or bit is too large or too small, and that even by punching more holes it still cannot be made to fit. The only answer here is to beg, borrow or buy another.

Many saddles are in poor condition. Make sure that the saddle is correctly stuffed, fits the horse, and does not pinch the withers or press upon the spine. Do not ride if the horse is galled.

(1), (2) and (3) indicate that training has been inadequate or wrongly carried out. This will often prove to be the case when a new horse is purchased.

Make a start with (1) and follow the instructions for "Loose Jumping" in *Training the Young Horse and Pony*. If all goes well assume that the horse has been overfaced as in (2) or frightened

FIGURE 14. FENCES WHICH ARE TOO BIG

as in (3) by falls or by hurting himself. Often it is the rider who is feeling nervous! Therefore lower the fences, laying poles on the ground at first, and get the horse going freely, only raising the fences again very gradually. When schooling, it is always advisable to keep the fences small so that the horse will jump anything the rider asks him to. Horses will invariably jump bigger fences out hunting or in competitions, provided they have been properly schooled, than they do at home in cold blood.

Sometimes a lead from another horse will give the necessary confidence, especially over a fence which cannot be lowered. If the animal is just idle or bored it is better to keep to low fences; wake him up by riding more vigorously and by schooling with another horse or, if old enough, take him hunting.

Lastly, there is the long whip in the hands of an assistant; this is certainly effective with some unwilling horses, but it is apt to frighten the rider more than the horse and what is gained by the one is lost by the other. Loud shouts are to be deprecated; better to lower the fence—or change the rider.

Rushing

A keen horse is apt to develop the habit of rushing his fences. In this case he should not be schooled over a series of fences in line ahead. Rather should he be ridden in a circle close to a single fence. When he is going quietly, the circle may unobtrusively be enlarged to include the fence, which he will probably take quite calmly. If he does not, reduce the size of the circle and miss the fence until he is quiet again.

In the case of a horse who "hots up" when he sees a course of show or schooling fences, he should be circled quietly among them until he has settled down, when the circle is varied as before to include a fence. Sometimes a horse will jump more calmly at a double, which has the effect of making him look carefully and lower his head.

A frequent cause of rushing is the action of the rider in taking a pull or a tighter hold of the horse's head in front of a fence. In this case the rider must learn to keep his hands steady and not to increase the pull on the reins. It is surprising how often a loose rein will cure this fault.

FIGURE 15.   A.   RUSHING HIS FENCES

FIGURE 16.   B.   TAKING HIS FENCES CALMLY

GATES

OPENING AND SHUTTING

Many people imagine that the hunting whip must be used to open and shut a gate. Consequently they get themselves into great difficulties. Whenever possible the hand should be used and the whip should only be resorted to when the gate or catch cannot be reached.

The horse's head should always be turned in the direction of the latch and the hand nearest the gate used.

To close the gate, turn the horse round and push the gate to. Make the horse stand parallel and close to the gate, while you lean down to fix the latch with the hand nearest the latch, having previously transferred the whip and reins to the other hand.

Practice

If horse and rider are not well trained to open and shut gates, much time will be lost when hounds are running. When passing through a swinging gate in a crowd, do not let the gate slam in front of the person following you but push it well back so that it comes nicely to hand.

If riding a horse that is liable to kick in a gateway, try to keep him moving forward. If this is not possible in the middle, it may be on a flank. It is asking for trouble to stand still, with your hand behind your back, waiting for people to move. A red ribbon is no excuse for kicking anybody.

HUNTING

This subject is dealt with in the Pony Club Publications "Five-Minute Lectures—Foxhunting", by W. W. B. Scott, "Riding to Hounds", by C. G. Cubitt, and the Film Strip Book, "Fox-hunting".

APPENDIX I

DRESSAGE

A SYSTEM OF BASIC TRAINING

Aims and objects

If the rider takes a great deal of trouble in the initial stages of training, he will reap great benefits as time goes on, because in order to be a good ride a horse must go correctly in all paces. The system of training recommended here will benefit all horses and is essential for those that are being trained for Combined Training and Dressage Events.

Our aim and object is that the horse should learn what is necessary in order to become a good all-round riding horse and hunter.

The horse should go freely forward with an even rhythm. He must be "on the bit" at all paces. He must have a steady, correct head-carriage, be in balance, straight, supple and completely obedient to the rider's aids.

Let us consider how these aims can be achieved. It is wishful thinking to imagine this high standard of training can be achieved in a short time. It is not possible, and any short cut taken by the use of auxiliary reins, etc., will show itself in many different ways. Any restriction or force used will result in shortened paces and, more than likely, incorrect head-carriage. For instance, should the rider use a martingale in order to hold the horse's head down, having it so fitted that the horse can "lean" against it, the horse will be using the wrong muscles in his neck and will miss it the moment it is removed. Consequently he will throw up his head, feeling for the strap which is not there, all of which will have aggravated a fault which will take long to correct.

If a young horse is inclined to throw his head up into a dangerous position, it is advisable to use a standing martingale, properly fitted so that it only comes into action when the horse has thrown his head up beyond the point of control. Fitted in this way, it acts only as a safeguard for the rider and in no way hinders the horse's training. The use of a running martingale for this purpose is unwise, as it influences the reins and causes a false action on the horse's mouth.

The rider must plan the schooling of his horse and the plan must be strictly adhered to. It is most important that the horse should become proficient in one stage before taken on to the next. This point must be stressed, because the horse has to learn to know what the aids mean. If great care is taken to make the aids clear and correct, the horse will soon learn what is wanted of him; but if he is hurried and the aids are not clear, he will get muddled, hot up and go back in his training.

FIRST STAGE

Rhythm

A horse must learn to stand still when being mounted. It should be the first lesson in obedience and the rider must be very strict about this. He should get off every time the horse moves, remount, and only give the aid to move on when the horse has stood perfectly still.

The horse must learn to go forward to the slightest pressure of the rider's leg-aid. If at first the horse does not respond, the rider can use a fairly long switch with which to touch him behind the girth, at the same time as he gives the leg-aid to "go forward". The horse will soon learn this aid and when he will go forward to the lightest pressure of the rider's legs, the stick need no longer be used.

The horse should trot forward at a brisk, controlled pace, with as long a stride as possible. Should he at any time quicken his pace, he must be brought back to a slower pace and then be asked again gradually to lengthen his stride (see figure 17). Each time he quickens or loses rhythm, the pace must be reduced and the exercise repeated. The amount of forward impulsion created should be determined by the temperament of the horse. Whereas the free-going horse would probably go naturally forward with long strides, the slow, lazy horse will need to be kept going forward by the use of the rider's legs and seat. The rider must at all times maintain a light, smooth and even contact with the horse's mouth.

At this stage the correct head-carriage will involve the neck being long and stretched and the head being in front of the perpendicular.

FIGURE 17.   LENGTHENING THE STRIDE

Positioning the head

We must now study how to get the horse's head in the correct position. If the horse carries his head too high, he must be "asked" to bring it down. Nothing is gained by the use of force, because the moment the force is relaxed, the head will once more take the false high position. Most horses are stiffer one side than the other, which means they resist more to one side than they do to the other. Therefore they are slightly more bent one way, because the muscles are shorter on the side to which they are bent than on the other side. In order to get the horse going straight, the muscles on the short (soft) side must be lengthened, so as to be the same as those on the resisting side.

No. **1.** *The horse answering the rein on the "soft" side.*

No. **2.** *The horse resisting the rein on the "hard" side.*

FIGURE 18.   FINDING THE HORSE'S STIFF SIDE

Illustrations reproduced from the book *Play the Game Riding* by Mrs. V.D.S. Williams. Published by EP Publishing Limited, Wakefield, England, © Copyright 1976, 1970.

In order to ascertain which is the stiff side, the rider should walk the horse on a loose rein, then pick up the left rein only (see No. 1 page 58), and if the horse answers immediately by turning his head to the left and moving off in that direction, it is almost certain that this is the soft side. If the rider now drops the left rein and picks up the right rein and he finds that the horse will not turn his head to the right, but moves in that direction with a stiff jaw and neck, keeping his head straight or even turning it slightly to the left (see figure 18, No. 2, page 58), then the right side is the stiff side. Having established this fact, the rider sets about "asking" the horse to lower his head (if it is too high) and relax his jaw.

FIGURE 19. THE HORSE MUST BE "ASKED" TO LOWER HIS HEAD

Illustrations reproduced from the book *Play the Game Riding* by Mrs. V.D.S. Williams. Published by EP Publishing Limited, Wakefield, England, © Copyright 1976, 1970.

He proceeds at the trot as described and takes a light but firm contact with the left rein (soft side). This contact must be kept throughout the lesson, no matter in which direction he is going. Now, by a slight tightening of the fingers on the right rein (stiff side) he "asks" for a relaxation of the horse's jaw and a consequent lowering of the head (see figure 19, No. 2). The motion is like "squeezing-water-out-of-a-sponge" and must not in any way be backwards. At the same time as the rider "asks" with his right hand, he also uses his legs, the right leg giving a stronger aid than the left. If this is repeated every time the horse gets his head too high, he will soon learn to lower it and relax his jaw (see figure 19). If the horse is stiff on the left side, the aids are, of course, reversed.

In the case of too low a head-carriage, the rider must use his legs to push the horse's head up, by making the hind-legs more active (see figure 20). The rider must never attempt to pull the head up with the hands, as the result would be a false head-carriage, with the top of the neck bent in a concave position, which is very damaging to the training. Carrying the head up in this position has the effect of hollowing the horse's back and thus making it impossible for him to use his back correctly or to bring his hind-legs under him. While the rider is teaching his horse to hold his head correctly, he must also concentrate on getting him into the habit of keeping it in this position when changing direction or altering pace. He must also remember to keep his horse trotting on in the same cadence, with a long stride.

FIGURE 20.   THE RIDER MUST "PUSH" THE HORSE'S HEAD UP

Illustrations reproduced from the book *Play the Game Riding* by Mrs. V.D.S. Williams. Published by EP Publishing Limited, Wakefield, England, © Copyright 1976, 1970.

A horse is a creature of habit. He nearly always does the same thing in the same place. It is the artist who understands this and can anticipate a fault, correcting it before it has, in fact, appeared.

Position of the head during transitions

At this stage the horse must be asked to reduce his pace from trot to walk very carefully and slowly. If he is hurried in any way, up will go the head again with the same false bend of the neck, causing a great deal of resistance in the mouth and back; or he might just catch hold of the bit and "lie" on it. In order to get a smooth reduction of pace, the rider closes both legs, sits very deep in the saddle, whilst he lightly resists with the hands and "asks" with the right hand and right leg (in this case), for a relaxation of the jaw and, as the horse responds, the rider must instantaneously be still with his hands and gently push the horse into a walk with his legs. The secret lies in "asking" and rewarding by the *immediate* relaxation of the aid when the horse has responded.

From a walk, the horse must be brought back to a halt, using exactly the same aids as when going from a trot into a walk. It is important for the horse to be made to stand squarely, equally balanced on all four legs. If one hind-leg is left behind, the rider can gently tap this leg with a switch, while giving a gentle aid with his leg on the same side. The horse will gradually learn to answer and bring up the hind-leg the moment he is asked. This will soon become a habit and he will adopt this stance on his own. It is sometimes difficult to feel which hind-leg is left behind, without looking down. As a guide, one should remember that whichever fore-leg is the last to move, it will be the opposite hind-leg which will need to be moved up. The horse must stand perfectly still until given the aid to move forward.

Practically every horse will alter the position of his head or change the length of his stride when changing direction or pace. The intelligent rider will anticipate this by preparing the horse for a change. He "asks" on the stiff side with his hand and leg *before* changing direction or pace, as much as to say: "Pay attention, I am going to do something different".

Until the horse will go forward with a level stride at a trot, change direction and come back to a walk without resisting or throwing up his head, he must not be taken on to the next stage. Large circles may be ridden but still the rider must demand nothing more than a level pace, a light mouth and obedience in going forward to the leg-aids.

SECOND STAGE

The canter

The horse should now be ready to learn to strike off into a canter. As the canter is a pace of three-time, the "Laterals" on the side to which he is cantering (that is, the leading fore-leg and the hind-leg on the same side) are slightly in advance of the other fore-leg and hind-leg, and therefore the horse should be slightly bent towards his leading fore-leg. If he is bent correctly going round a left-hand corner (which means he is slightly curved to the left), and then given the aids to canter, by the rider drawing back his right leg and creating a strong pressure with *both* legs, seat and back muscles, the horse will go quite naturally into a left canter. It is important here to draw particular attention to the use of *both* the rider's legs, together with the seat and back muscles. A horse will very quickly learn this aid. If the rider gets slack about using the aid correctly and eventually just brings back his leg, together with the use of the opposite rein, he will find himself in difficulties when, in the future training, he wants to teach his horse lateral work. The aids being much the same the rider must make himself very clear to his horse, or he will find that on asking for a half-pass the horse goes into a canter.

In the early stages the canter should be brisk and long, without collection, but with the same light contact with the horse's mouth. Should the horse start to "lie" on the bit, he must be given a half-halt by a strong use of the rider's back, seat and leg-aids, and then allowed to continue. If he puts up any resistance to one side, the same "giving-and-taking" movement can be applied with the rein on the "stiff" side, as has been described above. If there is no particular resistance to one side or the other, but just a general "lying on the bit", the "giving-and-taking" hand should be the one on the opposite side to the leading leg.

Only if the horse's hind-legs are active is it possible to get a balanced horse "sitting" on his hocks at the canter. Here again it is important to stress the tremendous power of the rider's back-aid. With this aid, and a slight resistance of the hands, the rider can "push the horse's quarters under him". This should be done gradually, until the horse will take up the position on his own account and become lightly balanced, while cantering on freely. With practice, the rider will come to feel the horse relaxing his back muscles, and the moment this happens he must sit still until he feels the back hard and resisting again. Then he must repeat the aid until gradually the horse remains cantering in a soft, relaxed position.

In order to bring the horse quietly back to a trot from a canter, the rider straightens his spine and holds the horse with his legs, whilst resisting slightly with the hand on the "soft" side and "asking" with the other hand. This transition should be practised continually so as to get it smooth, with no resistance or upward movement of the horse's head. Gradually it will be found that the moment the rider sits deep, closes his legs, and "asks" with the hand on the stiff side, the horse will come straight back into a correct trot stride and continue with a soft mouth, without any more resistance from the reins being necessary.

FIGURE 21. HOW TO STRAIGHTEN THE SPINE
TRANSITION FROM CANTER TO TROT

Placing the horse "on the bit"

The horse should now be ready to be put "on the bit", and to stay on it. Up to now we have only asked for a relaxation of the jaw and that the horse should go with a very light contact with the bit. Now, using the same methods as before (i.e., the "squeezing-water-out-of-a-sponge" movement, whenever a resistance is put up) the horse must be made not only to relax the jaw, but to hold the bit softly in his mouth with a light contact and remain in this position at all paces and in all directions.

In order to trot correctly the horse must "swing" his back and be active with his hind-legs. Unless he can do this, it is impossible for him to get round a corner smoothly or to perform a circle correctly. When making a circle, the horse's inside lateral legs must take a shorter stride than the outside laterals. If he is stiff and does not use his back, he cannot bend his hocks enough to keep the hind feet following exactly the imprints made by the fore-feet. Therefore he throws them out and they perform a larger circle than the fore-legs.

Suppling the horse

To overcome this the rider can supple his horse by means of various exercises. To supple the horse from front to rear, he performs a series of half-halts, obtained in the same manner as described above when coming from a trot to a walk; only in this case the horse is asked to trot on again just before breaking into a walk. The best method of suppling a horse laterally is to perform a shoulder-in. The importance of this exercise is that the horse must bend his spine, and by so doing flex his hocks, which can then be brought more underneath him. It is useless if he bends his neck only, which is undoubtedly what he will try to do. Because he finds it difficult to bend at the spine, he will try to create the illusion that he is doing so by bending his neck only, and thus evade the exercise. This will do more harm than good, because if he is allowed to make this evasion he will, in time, become what is called "rubber-necked". The term is self-explanatory and the fault very difficult to correct.

To perform a right shoulder-in the horse's forehand is taken off the tracks as if about to start a circle, but instead of continuing the circle the rider's inside (right) leg, held at the girth, pushes the horse's forehand to the left, so that the horse will continue going forward with the head, neck and spine following a curve of which the centre is the rider's right leg. At the same time the rider keeps the horse's hind legs on the track, and his quarters from going to the left, by bringing his left leg back behind the girth, thus controlling the quarters and maintaining the impulsion (see figure 22).

The easiest way to start a shoulder-in is on a bend. Coming round the corner the rider applies the above aids and, instead of straightening out after the corner, he holds this position. If the horse responds by performing just two steps sideways, the pressure of the inside leg should immediately be relaxed and the horse allowed to go forward into a large half-circle. It is better to continue on a circle than to bring the forehand back on to the track, because the horse being already bent in the direction of the circle, should be allowed to do the easiest movement as a reward for having responded to the aid. Very gradually the horse must be asked to do more and more steps at the shoulder-in until, with the greatest of ease, he will perform this exercise to either hand for quite long stretches.

This exercise is best performed at a trot, but sometimes it is easier to teach the horse to understand the aids first at a walk. However, as soon as the horse understands what is required of him it should not be performed at a walk again. The better the movement, the better the exercise and it is dangerous to do too much work at the walk, except on a long rein, as the horse will lose impulsion and can more easily produce evasions and get behind the bit.

There can be different degrees of shoulder-in. It is better to get the horse moving on two different tracks so that, while the hind-legs continue on one track, the fore-legs follow a line parallel to them (see right shoulder-in, figure 22 below), because in this way the rider will get more flexibility of the spine and more activity in the hind legs. At first the rider can ask for only a small bend, so that the inside hind-leg follows the track made by the outside fore-leg;

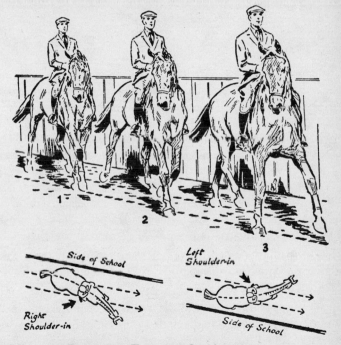

FIGURE 22. THE RIGHT SHOULDER-IN

Illustrations reproduced from the book *Play the Game Riding* by Mrs. V.D.S. Williams. Published by EP Publishing Limited, Wakefield, England, © Copyright 1976, 1970.

but the rider must be quite certain that the horse is in this position and not just bending his neck. No force must be used in this exercise and it must not be performed if the horse's head is too high. The head and neck must remain still and in the correct position. To perform the left shoulder-in, the aids are reversed.

In order to appreciate the importance of the shoulder-in as a suppling exercise, it should be realised that it is the easiest way in which to make a horse straight, because it makes him bend his spine on the stiff side and activates the hind-legs, which otherwise he would not attempt to do.

Circles

It is now time to ask for more correctness in the horse's movements. To ride a circle correctly, the horse's spine should comply with the direction of the movement and follow the circumference of the circle. It is easy for a spectator to see if a horse is correct or not, because his hind-feet should follow exactly in the tracks made by the fore-feet. They may be on or over them according to the pace at which the horse is going, but not to one side or the other. It has been made clear why it is so necessary to ask only large circles during the early stages of training. The smaller the circle the more active must be the hind-legs, in order that they bend enough to follow the tracks made by the fore-feet.

It is interesting to assess the progress and accuracy of the training by riding a circle on ground upon which the imprints of the horse's hoofs can be seen.

A horse must always look to the way he is going (except in the shoulder-in). If performing a circle to the right, he must be bent in a curve round the rider's right leg, and if going to the left, he must be bent round the left leg (see figure 23). A horse should follow the direction in which his head is pointing. That is why it is so necessary to be as accurate as possible when riding through corners during the early stages of training.

The rider must be careful to see that the horse remains on the bit during the whole circle. Any exercise incorrectly performed should be repeated again and again until it is done correctly. Then make much of the horse before continuing with another exercise, or give him a rest by walking on a long rein.

FIGURE 23.   THE HORSE MUST CHANGE THE BEND AS HE CHANGES DIRECTION

Illustrations reproduced from the book *Play the Game Riding* by Mrs. V.D.S. Williams. Published by EP Publishing Limited, Wakefield, England, © Copyright 1976, 1970.

The turn on the forehand

In order to get control of the horse's quarters and to be sure he will go away from the rider's leg, the Turn on the Forehand can be taught. This exercise is a means to an end, and when achieved there is no necessity to use it again. The horse is placed alongside, but not too near, a fence or wall. He must be standing squarely on all four legs and be holding the bit lightly in his mouth. It is most important not to attempt to start this exercise if there is any resistance whatsoever in the horse's mouth. To turn to the right on the forehand, the rider gently "asks" with the right rein, but should not turn the horse's head more than just enough to make his right eye visible. With the right leg drawn back behind the girth he pushes the horse's quarters over to the left. The rider's left leg remains at the girth to keep him from stepping backwards and to help send him forward the moment the turn is completed (see figure 24). It is not a good thing to halt after a turn on the forehand because this is apt to cause loss of forward impulsion, and the horse can easily put up an evasion by getting behind the bit.

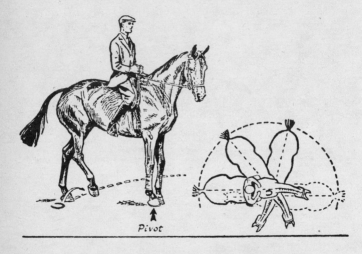

Pivot

FIGURE 24.   THE RIGHT TURN ON THE FOREHAND

Illustrations reproduced from the book *Play the Game Riding* by Mrs. V.D.S. Williams. Published by EP Publishing Limited, Wakefield, England, © Copyright 1976, 1970.

In the turn to the right the off-fore is the pivotting leg, which can either actually pivot, or be picked up and put down again in the same place. The horse's off-hind-leg should cross over in front of the near-hind. He must on no account step backwards. To start with, only two steps should be asked and the horse sent forward again; the rider gradually asking more and more until a full half-turn can be made without any resistance from the horse and with a perfectly still head-carriage.

THIRD STAGE

The rider

It is impossible to lay down any hard or fast rule for training a horse and this is only meant as a guide. Some horses take much longer than others, so it is impossible to give any specific time. But if the work so far has been correct, the horse should by now be permanently "on the bit", which means he is holding it lightly in his mouth, with a relaxed jaw and obeying the aids without resistance. Naturally there will always be moments when the horse puts up an evasion and resists the bit, but he should respond immediately to a correction given. If he does not obey, and if there is no obvious reason, like excitement caused by another horse, a car going down the road, or a bird suddenly flying up, then the rider must ask himself why, and what has been wrong with his training. It may be that he uses too much hand and not enough leg. It may be that he is stiff himself, which will communicate itself at once to the horse, with dire results. Or it may be that he has not been clear enough with his aids.

It is very important for the rider to analyse himself and to be sure he is sitting correctly. If he is getting too far forward, he will not be in a position to give correct aids. If he is sitting in the shape of a bow, it would be impossible for him to use his back to push the horse forward. If he loses his temper he will never get anywhere. So, if things go wrong, the rider must not blame the horse but himself, and correct his position if necessary.

Every day the rider must go over all these exercises we have discussed. As time goes on, he must ask for a better and better performance, aiming always towards perfection. He must be more strict with the not-so-good movements. If the rider is satisfied with the progress his horse has made, he may now take his training on a further step by teaching him to counter-canter.

The counter-canter

This is also an excellent suppling exercise, but it must not be attempted too early as, until the horse is fairly supple he cannot perform it correctly and he will start changing legs behind, which is a very difficult habit to cure.

First try rather long and not very deep serpentines at the canter. For instance, canter in a school or alongside a fence on the right leg; then bring the horse off the track and return to the track without changing legs. The rider must remember to keep the horse bent to the right, even when going to the left, as it is important for him to keep the bend towards the leading leg. As the horse gets more and more supple, these serpentines can get deeper and deeper, until the rider can take his horse round a school in a counter-canter and finally perform a complete circle. (This means going round to the left with the right leg leading, or vice versa.) Progress must be very gradual, and the rider must be content with a little at a time. It is far better to go slowly and get it right, than to hurry in the early stages and then later have to correct other faults which have been produced by "forcing the pace". Naturally the exercise must be practised equally on both reins.

The counter-canter must not be confused with the disunited canter, which is an evasion and is always incorrect. In the true canter, one pair of laterals (both legs on one side) should be in advance of the other pair (see above, under the heading "The Canter"). In the disunited canter, the horse is leading with the near-fore and the off-hind, or vice versa.

The walk from the canter

The next exercise to teach the horse is the canter-to-walk. This must only be attempted if the rider is quite sure the horse will answer his seat aids and relax his back muscles by producing more active hock action. If the horse is at all stiff in the back, the rider will not be able to get a correct canter-to-walk and much resistance and throwing up of the horse's head will result, all of which will be very detrimental to the horse's training.

It is best to start this movement on a fairly large circle, as the horse finds it easier to be balanced at the canter when not on a straight line. Whilst keeping the horse bent slightly to the leading leg, the rider closes his legs, sits very deep and well down in the saddle and, by using strong seat and back-aids, supported by closed legs into resisting hands, pushes the horse's hind-legs more and more underneath him, until the horse's balance is such that he can pass straight into a walk. This will not be accomplished the first time it is attempted, because it is probable that the horse will not be sufficiently in balance and will therefore have to take two or three steps at a trot. If the rider's aids are not clear or strong enough, the horse will come back with his weight on his forehand. The rider must make the horse canter more and more slowly by lowering the croup, and thus making him light in hand. Only then can the horse pass straight into a walk. As soon as the horse walks, the reins must immediately be relaxed and the horse allowed to walk freely on without any restriction.

The simple change

When the foregoing movement has been successfully achieved, the rider may attempt a simple change of leg, but it is most important to get the canter-to-walk first. It is also necessary before starting this exercise, to be sure that the horse will strike off into a canter on either leg on a straight line and be perfectly straight while doing so. It would be a mistake to try a simple change of leg if the horse throws his quarters in when striking off into a canter, as it would only aggravate this fault and then there would be many difficulties to overcome in order to get a correct change of leg. The reason for correct canter-aids is now obvious.

If the rider's inside leg and seat are used to the same extent as the outside leg, the horse will not learn this annoying habit of pushing his quarters to the inside when striking off into a canter, and there will be no need for any corrections.

To practise the simple change of leg at the canter:— Canter off on a named leg, perform a canter-to-walk and walk on for some distance before striking off on the other leg. Gradually reduce the length of walk in between the canters until there are only two or three paces at the walk. The resulting simple change of leg will have been performed with the greatest of ease.

This is the correct simple change of leg; but in all dressage tests up to Medium class this change can be done progressively through a trot. There must, however, always be a few paces performed at the walk.

Conclusion

If this system of training is carefully adhered to, so that all resistance is reduced to a minimum before any difficult exercise is asked, the rider will find these exercises falling into his lap, like a ripe plum does from a tree, directly the horse understands what is required of him. Because, having taught the horse obedience and how to relax, the rider does not have the dual task of teaching him simultaneously a new aid, and overcoming a resistance. The secret is obedience—the proud result of correct training, which has caused the horse to give himself willingly and to obey with pleasure the indications of the rider. This training will have developed the horse's muscles and suppled him, to such an extent as to make jumping easier. It will also have got him into the habit of obedience, which will go a long way towards eliminating the possibility of refusals when jumping.

APPENDIX II

DRESSAGE
DEFINITIONS OF TERMS AND MOVEMENTS

Objects of Dressage

The true purpose of dressage is to improve the standard of training of the riding horse and to provide a progressive system which will teach the horse to balance himself with the weight of his rider, without putting undue strain on any sets of joints or muscles, thus enabling him to comply easily and happily with the demands of his rider and to improve his paces and bearing.

The whole secret of dressage lies in placing the horse's head in the right position by controlling the hind legs. It is the rider's legs and seat that must be the chief influence in placing the horse's head, and a snaffle bridle is the only bit for the purpose. If an attempt is made to pull the horse's head into position with a double bridle, the mouth would inevitably be ruined and the action impaired. The double bridle should not be used until the position of the head is established.

The horse must be made to go forward by the hind legs propelling the fore legs immediately in front of them. He must be taught to increase and decrease his stride in all paces without altering the rhythm. He must be taught the lateral movements, not only to enable him to go on two tracks, but in order to overcome evasions, to supple the spine, to teach the horse to be obedient to the rider's legs and to keep the horse straight.

The greatest difficulty in equitation is to keep the horse straight.

Rhythm

The ordered flow of movement—the regularity and evenness of the hoofbeat.

On the bit

At the halt and when on the move, the horse must be on the bit except when on a loose rein.

A horse is said to be "on the bit" when the hocks are correctly placed, the neck is more or less raised according to the collection or extension of the pace, the head remains steadily in position, the contact with the mouth is light and no resistance is offered to the rider.

Loose rein

When there is no influence by the rider's hands on the bit.

Bit evasions

A term used to express the fact that the horse does not go "on the bit" when required to do so.

Bit evasions include:—

(1) *Tongue over the bit*. The horse's tongue lies above the bar of the bit.

(2) *Tongue drawn back towards the throat*. The horse rolls his tongue up behind the bar of the bit.

(3) *Over the bit*. The horse leans too much on the bit.

(4) *Above the bit*. The horse raises his head with a stiff poll and takes the pressure of the bit on the lips instead of on the bars of the mouth.

(5) *Behind the bit*. The horse drops the bit by bringing his mouth in towards his chest.

PACES

Extracts from the Rules of the Federation Equestre Internationale

Steps, strides, paces

There are four steps to a stride at the pace of the walk (4-time).
There are two steps to a stride at the pace of the trot (2-time).
There are three steps to a stride at the pace of the canter (3-time).
There are two steps to a stride at the pace of the rein back (2-time).
There are four steps to a stride at the pace of the gallop (4-time).

Halt

At the halt the horse should stand attentive, motionless and straight, with the weight evenly distributed over all four legs and be ready to move off at the slightest indication of the rider. The neck should be raised, the poll high, the head a little in front of the vertical, the mouth light, the horse champing his bit and maintaining a light contact with the rider's hand.

The transition from any pace to the halt should be made progressively in a smooth and precise movement.

The walk

The walk is a marching pace in which the four legs of the horse follow one another in four time, with the cadence well marked and maintained. When the four beats cease to be well marked, even and regular, the walk is disunited or broken.

It is at the pace of the walk that the imperfections in dressage are most marked. The pace will suffer if the degree of collection is not in accordance with the stage of schooling of the horse, but is precipitated.

The following walks are recognised: ordinary, collected, extended and free.

Ordinary walk

A free, regular and unconstrained walk of moderate extension. The horse should walk energetically but calmly, with even and determined steps, distinctly marking four equally-spaced beats. The rider should keep a light and steady contact with the mouth.

Collected walk

The horse moves resolutely forward, with his neck raised and arched. The head approaches the vertical position, the light contact with the mouth being maintained. The hind legs are engaged with good hock action. The pace should remain marching and vigorous, the legs being placed in regular sequence. Each step covers less ground and is higher than at the ordinary walk because all the joints bend more markedly. The hind feet touch the ground behind the footprints of the fore feet.

In order not to become hurried or irregular the collected walk is slightly shorter than the ordinary walk, although showing greater mobility.

Extended walk

The horse should cover as much ground as possible, without haste and without losing the regularity of his steps. The hind feet touch the ground clearly beyond the footprints of the fore-feet. The rider lets the horse stretch out his head and neck without however, losing contact, the head being carried in front of the vertical.

Free walk

The free walk is a pace of rest in which, the reins being stretched to their utmost, the horse is allowed complete freedom of his head and neck.

The trot

The trot is a pace of two-time on alternate diagonals (near fore and off hind, and vice versa) separated by a moment of suspension.

The trot, always with free, active and regular steps, should be moved into without hesitation.

The quality of the trot is judged by the general impression, the elasticity and regularity of the steps and the impulsion, while maintaining the same cadence.

The following trots are recognised: ordinary, collected and extended.

Ordinary trot

This is a pace between the extended and the collected trot. The horse goes forward freely and straight, engaging his hind legs with good hock action, on a taut but light rein, his position being balanced and unconstrained. The steps should be as even as possible. The hind feet touch the ground in the footprints of the forefeet.

The degree of energy and impulsion displayed at the ordinary trot denotes clearly the degree of suppleness and balance of the horse.

Collected trot

The neck is raised, thus enabling the shoulders to move with greater ease, the hocks being well engaged and maintaining energetic impulsion, notwithstanding the slower movement. The horse's steps are shorter, but he is lighter and more mobile.

Extended trot

The horse covers as much ground as possible. He lengthens his stride, remaining on the bit with light contact. The neck is extended and, as a result of great impulsion from the quarters, the horse uses his shoulders, covering more ground at each step without his action becoming much higher.

The ordinary trot and extended trot are executed "rising". The collected trot is executed "sitting" unless otherwise instructed.

The canter

The canter is a pace of three-time. In the right canter for instance, the sequence is as follows: left hindleg, left diagonal (right hind and left foreleg), right foreleg, followed by a period of suspension with all four legs in the air, before taking the next stride.

The following canters are recognised: ordinary, collected and extended.

Ordinary canter

This is a pace between the extended canter and the collected canter. The horse, perfectly straight from head to tail, moves freely, with a natural balance. The strides are long and even and the pace well cadenced. The quarters develop an increasing impulsion.

Collected canter

The shoulders are supple, free and mobile and the quarters very active. The horse's mobility is increased without any loss of impulsion.

Extended canter

The horse extends his neck; the tip of the nose points more or less forwards, the horse lengthens his stride without losing any of his calmness and lightness.

Counter canter (false canter)

This movement is a canter to the left with the off fore leading, or to the right with the near fore leading.

On the circle this is a suppling movement. The horse maintains his lateral flexion at the poll to the outside of the circle; in other words remains bent to the leading leg. His conformation does not permit his spine to be bent to the line of the circle.

The rider, avoiding any contortion causing contraction and discomfort, should especially endeavour to limit the deviation of the quarters to the outside and restrict his demands according to the degree of suppleness of the horse.

Simple change of leg at the canter

This is a change whereby the horse is brought back into a walk and, after one or two well defined steps, restarted into a canter with the other leg leading.

The change in the air—flying change of leg at the canter

The horse changes leg "in the air" in a single stride while cantering. This change of leg is termed as "flying" (or "in the air") when it is executed at the moment of suspension which follows each stride at the canter. The horse remains straight, calm and light.

The rein-back

The rein-back is the walk backwards, the legs being raised and set down simultaneously by diagonal pairs. It is correct when the horse moves regularly in two-time, the hindlegs remaining well in line and the legs being well raised.

The horse must be ready to halt or move forward without pausing, at the demand of his rider, remaining at all times lightly on the bit and well balanced.

Any signs of hurrying, evasion of the hand, deviation of the quarters from the straight line or spreading and inactivity of the haunches are serious faults. Violent influence on the part of the rider may be detrimental to the joints of the hind quarters. A horse that is not obedient to the aids of the rider in the rein-back is insufficiently suppled, badly schooled or badly ridden.

Submission

At all paces, a slight flexion of the jaw, without nervousness, is a criterion of the obedience of the horse and of the harmonious distribution of his forces. Grinding the teeth and swishing the tail are signs of resistance on the part of the horse.

TRANSITIONS

Change of pace and speed

Such changes should always be prompt but smooth and not abrupt. The cadence of a pace should be maintained up to the moment when the pace or speed is changed or the horse halts. The horse remains light in hand, calm and maintains a correct position.

Change of direction

At changes of direction the horse should adjust the bend of his body to the curvature of the line he follows, remaining supple and following the indications of the rider without any resistance or change of pace or speed.

Halt and half-halts

The halt signifies the manner of stopping the horse at the end of a movement. Consequently, halt means "stop".

The halt is obtained by a displacement of the weight on to the quarters by the action of the seat and by a resisting action of the hands, causing an instantaneous stop, while the legs are kept in readiness to maintain the impulsion.

The half-halt is an action of the hand with the object of preparing for the full halt or the transition to a lesser pace. In shifting more weight on the quarters, the engagement of the hind legs and balance on the haunches are facilitated.

LATERAL MOVEMENTS

Work on two tracks

The aim of the lateral movements is to bring the balance and the pace into harmony. They supple all parts of the horse, increasing especially the suppleness of the quarters and of the joints, and the freedom of the shoulders. They also make the horse more obedient to the aids of the rider.

The lateral movements should only be practised for a short time and always be followed by some energetic movement straight forward.

At the lateral movements the horse is bent uniformly from the poll to the tail towards the direction in which he is going and moves with the forehand and the quarters on two distinct tracks. The distance between the tracks should not be more than one step. The pace remains always regular, supple and free, maintained by a constant impulsion; this is often lost because the rider is pre-occupied with the bend of the horse only.

In work on two tracks the forehand should always be in advance of the quarters.

Shoulder-in

The horse is bent round the inside leg of the rider. The outside shoulder is placed in front of the inside hind quarter. The inside legs pass and cross in front of the outside legs. The horse's body is bent away from the direction to which he is moving.

The bend of the horse is more or less accentuated according to the degree of lateral suppleness the rider seeks to attain.

Half pass

The horse moves on two tracks, the head, neck and shoulders always slightly in advance of the quarters. A slight bend permitting the horse to look in the direction of the movement adds to his grace and gives more freedom of movement to the outside shoulder. The outside legs pass and cross in front of the inside legs. No slowing down of the pace is to be tolerated.

The legs on the side to which the horse is bent are the inside legs, those on the opposite side the outside legs.

The half pass can be demanded on the diagonal across the arena, in which case the horse must remain parallel to the long side of the school.

Turn on the forehand

In the turn on the forehand, the horse's quarters are moved in even, quiet and regular steps round the inner foreleg. The horse's head must remain in the correct position; the inner foreleg, acting as a pivot, should remain as nearly as possible on the same spot. This movement must only be done from the halt.

Half Pirouette

This is the half-turn on the haunches. The forehand commences the half-turn tracing a half-circle round the haunches, without pausing, at the moment the inside hind leg ceases its forward movement. The horse moves forward again, without a pause, upon completion of the half-turn.

During this movement the horse should maintain his impulsion and should never in the slightest move backwards or deviate sideways. It is necessary that the inside hind leg, while forming the pivot, should return to the same spot each time it leaves the ground.

Pirouette

This movement is a small circle on two tracks, with a radius equal to the length of the horse, the forehand moving round the haunches.

At whatever pace the pirouette is executed, the horse should turn smoothly, maintaining the exact cadence and sequence of legs of that pace.

At the pirouette, as at the half-pirouette, the forelegs and the outside hind leg move round the inside hind leg, which forms the pivot and should return to the same spot each time it leaves the ground. If, at the canter, this leg is not raised and returned to the ground in the same way as the other hindleg, the pace is no longer regular.

In executing the pirouette, the rider should maintain perfect lightness while accentuating the collection and the engagement of the quarters.

The quality of the pirouette is appreciated according to the regularity of the pace, its suppleness and cadence, the unobtrusiveness of the rider's aids, and the position and contact of the horse during and after the execution of the movement.

PART II.

SADDLERY

CARE

WELL-CLEANED and well-fitted saddlery adds much to the pleasing appearance and comfort of a pony and rider, whereas dirty, ill-fitting saddlery can be unsafe and detracts from both value and looks.

Knowledgeable horsemen or women will not use bad or coloured saddlery, neither will they neglect the care of the saddlery which they know plays such an influential part in good horsemanship.

Good saddlery needs the best leather and is therefore expensive. Good secondhand saddlery can be obtained but it is generally worth spending a little extra to buy new that will fit correctly. There are many comparatively cheap kinds on the market which, if bought, will prove unsatisfactory as regards comfort, suitability and wear and which might be the cause of an accident. There are also many fashionable bits and gadgets which can be tempting to buy but this book does not propose to discuss their merits. Many are for the use of the specialist, and here is set out only the requirements for general purpose riding. It is wise to obtain expert advice from an instructor when buying saddlery.

All saddlery, called "tack" in stable parlance, should be inspected periodically and minor defects attended to. Particular attention should be paid to the stitching, as the life of the thread is short compared with that of the leather. Stirrup leathers should occasionally be shortened from the buckle end so as to bring wear into fresh holes. A check must also be kept that bits do not become worn and rough.

Leather gets dry and cracks unless kept pliable with oil or fat. Thus it is necessary to soften it with a lubricant to replace the natural oil. Vegetable or animal oil such as castor oil, dubbin, neatsfoot oil or glycerine are good for leather. Linseed or mineral oil such as motor or bicycle oil are not as they become hard. However, the best kinds of saddle soap contain the necessary amount of glycerine or oil in order to keep saddlery that is in regular use pliable. Should it become necessary to store saddlery for any length of time, it is best to cover it with a thin coating of vaseline as this does not dry or decompose on exposure to air.

Leather must not be washed with soda or hot water, neither should it be placed close to a hot fire.

When the saddle and bridle are removed from the pony they should be hung up or put in a place of safety, allowing for air to get to the saddle lining. A saddle carelessly thrown down may result in a broken tree.

Materials required for tack cleaning

An apron or overall to save spoiling clothes.

A piece of rough towelling for washing.

A small flat sponge known as an "elephant ear sponge" for saddle soap, or a piece of foam rubber.

A chamois leather, for drying.

A tin or bar of glycerine saddle soap or plain saddle soap.

A tin of metal polish or impregnated polishing wool.

Two stable rubbers, one to cover the clean saddle, one for drying metal work.

A dandy brush, for brushing off sweat from serge linings.

Silver Sand, or a burnisher for plain steel.

An old cloth for applying polish and silver sand.

A nail or sharpened bit of wood to clean curb hooks and lip strap D's.

A duster for rubbing up after using metal polish.

A rubber or plastic bucket (that will not scratch metal) of cold or tepid water.

Hooks to hang bridle, girths, leathers, &c. on (*see figure* 27).

A saddle horse (*see figure* 28).

A vegetable oil for softening.

THE SADDLE

Structure

The frame that a saddle is built on is called a saddle-tree and is made of beech wood (*see figure* 25A). If a saddle is dropped or if a pony rolls with his saddle on, the tree may break and it will have to go to the saddler to be mended. A saddle with a broken tree will injure a pony's back, therefore, if there is any doubt it should be tested by a saddler. To be comfortable, a saddle should be shaped so as to assist the rider to sit in the centre and lowest part of the saddle.

On most stirrup bars there is a hinge that allows the point to be turned up. The purpose of this is to prevent the leathers slipping off when a saddled pony is being led without a rider. The points should never be up when the pony is being ridden (*see figure* 25A).

A saddle may have a full or half panel, and is stuffed with wool or shaped felt.

A full panel (*figure* 25D) reaches almost to the bottom of the saddle flap and is lined all the way down. It has only a short sweat-flap, sometimes called an underflap, between it and the girth tabs.

A half panel (*see figure* 25E) reaches half way down the saddle flap. It has a large sweat-flap reaching almost to the bottom of the saddle flap.

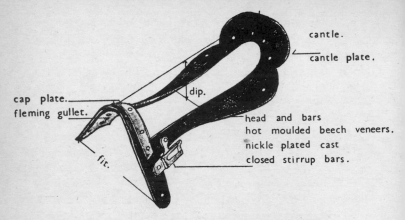

cantle.

cantle plate.

dip.

cap plate.
fleming gullet.

head and bars
hot moulded beech veneers.
nickle plated cast
closed stirrup bars.

fit.

FIGURE 25. A. THE PONY CLUB SADDLE TREE

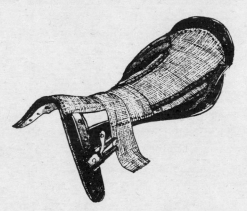

FIGURE 25. B. SADDLE TREE AFTER STRAINING

The rider's knee and lower part of the leg are closer to the pony in a half panel saddle.

A general purpose or jumping saddle may have a full panel, which is stuffed like a half panel saddle, is forward cut and has additional knee rolls on top of the panels.

FIGURE 25. c, d, e
FIGURE 25. THE PARTS OF A SADDLE

The Pony Club Saddle

The foundation of any saddle is the tree (*see figure* 25). If the tree is wrong the saddle is wrong. The tree approved by the Pony Club is marked on the stirrup bar "Pony Club Approved". It is made to a master pattern kept at Pony Club Headquarters.

If a saddle is the wrong shape, the rider will sit wrong in it, however good the leather, or lining.

Bands of webbing are stretched along the tree on which the stuffing and leather of the seat is carried— (*see figure* 25B). It must be neither too tight nor too loose if the seat of the saddle is to have the right dip and its deepest part in the right place. This is measured by a metal gauge issued on request to manufacturing saddlers, of which the master gauge is kept at Pony Club Headquarters. Various makers have submitted saddles for approval and these saddles are marked on the flap under the skirt "Pony Club Approved" and, of course, are made on an approved tree.

All saddles should be fitted to the pony to be absolutely perfect.

All sorts of variations and refinements can be applied to the standard saddle—leather lining, forward cut flaps, &c. If, as time goes on a child becomes so expert as to be able to take advantage of a special purpose saddle, he or she will, in a Pony Club approved saddle, have established a correct seat.

Linings

There are three kinds of saddle linings: linen, leather and serge.

Serge is absorbent but it does not wear well and is hard to keep clean.

Leather will last a long time if well kept and the saddle used frequently.

Linen is easy to wipe over to keep clean, dries quickly, wears much longer than serge but not so long as leather.

Fitting

The following points require attention when fitting a saddle:

(1) The weight of the saddle must be evenly distributed on the "lumbar" muscles, which cover the upper part of the ribs. There should be no weight on the loins.

   There must be no pressure on the pony's spine. It is important to pay attention to the back of a saddle when the rider is mounted. Pressure here often goes unnoticed. A sore or lump on the spine may lay a pony off for some considerable time.

(2) The withers must not be pinched (i.e. front arch too narrow) or pressed upon (i.e. front arch too low or too wide). All saddles tend to be lower on a pony's withers and back when he is thin (Christmas to Easter) than when he is fat (Summer).

(3) The play of the shoulder blades must not be hampered. Many saddle panels are incorrectly stuffed, causing the rider to lose contact with the mount. They should be so regulated as to give some support for the knee and be tilted so that the rider does not slide backwards, but remains in the centre of the saddle.

Many modern forward cut saddles, particularly those with a spring tree, concentrate too much pressure on a small portion of the panel beneath the stirrup bar. When buying or fitting a saddle, the size and width of the pony as well as the height of the rider should be considered. The size of the saddle is measured from the front of the pommel to the cantle (*see figure* 25c). According to the width of the pony the saddler is able to decide whether a wide, medium or narrow tree is required, or special stuffing. Any peculiarity such as a very prominent wither must also be noted.

To measure the width of a pony use half inch lead gas pipe or other malleable, non springy material, two feet long. Mould it over the withers three inches back from the shoulder where the front arch of the saddle should rest and then lift it off and pencil the (inside) shape on a piece of paper. This can also be sent to the saddler when re-stuffing an old saddle.

It is good practice to have a saddle looked over once a year by a saddler who will test the tree, stitching and re-stuff it if necessary.

The Pony Club approved saddle will be found to be a reasonable fit throughout the year for most ponies, and certainly cause no discomfort to the pony.

Standard and carrying

When placed on the ground a saddle should be stood on its front arch with the girth folded so as to protect the pommel from the rough ground.

A forward cut saddle will not rest on its front arch so when leant against a wall, etc., the girth should be folded along the gullet and over the cantle. An unprotected saddle leant against a wall or stood on a rough, hard surface will become worn and torn. Always put it down where it will not be knocked over by persons or ponies.

A saddle should be carried:—

(1) With the front arch in the crook of the elbow, which allows the bridle to be carried on the same shoulder, while the other hand is free for opening doors &c.; or (2) Along the thigh with the hand in the front arch. These methods prevent the cantle from being

scraped and cut against walls and when passing through doorways. A good saddle is something to be proud of and if treated with care will last a lifetime.

Cleaning

Place the saddle on the saddle horse. (For the ideal shape, see figure 28, where the saddle is held firm to the end of the panels.) It is a bad practice to clean or keep a saddle on the back of a chair or any sharp surface which causes the saddle to rock and rest on the gullet.

Strip the saddle, i.e. remove girths, stirrup-leathers and irons and girth buckle guards. Then clean the lining, which may be of leather, linen or serge.

If of leather, remove all dirt and dried sweat by holding the saddle, pommel down, over a bucket and wash with cold or luke-warm water. The saddle should be held so as to prevent water running under the lining and saturating the felt or stuffing. The lining should be dried with a chamois leather and then soaped with saddle soap. If the lining is of linen, sponge off, or scrub if necessary, keep as dry as possible and then stand the saddle up to dry. It must not, however, be placed too near a hot radiator or fire. If the lining is of serge, the saddle must be dried and then well brushed with a dandy brush. If it is very dirty it may be necessary to scrub it, but it will then take several days to dry.

The saddle should then be replaced on a saddle horse. Thoroughly wash with cold or tepid (not hot) water all the leather work, the seat, the outside and underneath of the flaps. Then dry off with the chamois leather, which is never used dry, but should be well wrung out. All small black accumulations of grease and dirt, known as "jockeys", should have been removed. If they are difficult to remove they will rub off with a small pad of horse hair.

On no account should any sharp instrument be used. Now with the sponge (kept for soaping) used as dry as possible, soap liberally with a circular movement. If the bar type soap is used dip the end of the bar in tepid water, and then rub the soap on to the sponge. If the sponge lathers it is too wet. Soap all accessible surfaces—the under side of the flaps and sweat flaps which is the flesh side of the leather, and therefore the most absorbent, should be most liberally soaped. Never use soap on top of dirt. If vegetable oil is used to soften do not use it on the seat or the outside of the flaps as it will stain the rider's breeches. Do not polish the saddle after soaping. Before using it again the seat and outside of the flaps can be rubbed over with a moist sponge and dried off with a chamois leather in order to remove all surplus soap which has not worked in and which could also stain breeches. The stirrup irons should be removed from the leathers and washed and dried. Leathers and girths hung up, on a cleaning bracket. An ideal bracket is suspended away from the wall (*see figure* 27) and can consist of many hooks tied together like an anchor with some hooks small enough to take a girth buckle. The stirrup leathers, girth (if leather) and buckle guards should be treated in the same way as the saddle, washed, dried and soaped. Again care should be taken not to have the sponge too wet or lather will fill the holes of the stirrup leathers which, if not kept clean with a match or nail, will accumulate dirt.

Clean all metal work with metal polish and duster. Now cover the saddle with a stable rubber and all is ready to be "put up" in a dry place.

Putting up

A simple and tidy way of "putting up" a saddle is to have a peg, or bracket, made for the purpose, about 18 in. long, attached to the wall of the saddle room at a convenient height. Place the saddle, front arch to the wall, on the peg. Have a hook underneath the peg on which to hang the stirrup irons. Have four other hooks placed on the wall on each side of the saddle, on which can be hung the girth, the stirrup leathers, and martingale. It is better for the girth and leathers to be put up hanging straight. Leathers should be constantly checked to be sure that they have not stretched and that their holes are level.

Figure 26 shows a saddle "put up" with a martingale on the left, and the girth and leathers on the right. See also figure 28: a saddle ready for use on the saddle horse.

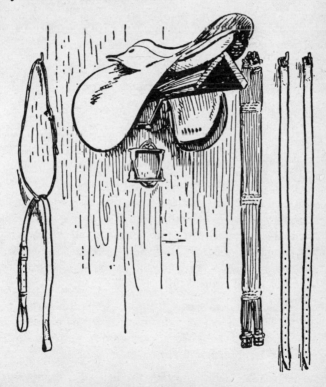

FIGURE 26. A SADDLE "PUT-UP"

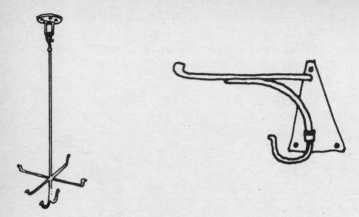

FIGURE 27.   TACK CLEANING BRACKETS

THE NUMNAH OR PAD SADDLE

Characteristics

A pad saddle is made of felt. Some are covered or partially covered with leather. It has either no tree or only a tree forepart. The pad saddle is better with a tree forepart or steel arch because it will sit straight on the pony, and assist the rider to sit correctly. A crupper may be necessary when the pad is used on a fat pony with round back and withers.

These saddles frequently have their own web girth permanently attached to the saddle on one side and fastened by one strap and buckle on the other. For safety they should have two straps and buckles or preferably two web girths.

Some pad saddles are fitted with "D's" instead of proper stirrup bars. These are dangerous, as also is any device which prevents the stirrup leather coming off the bar if pulled back. If such is used, safety stirrups should be employed. These "D's" are usually found on a saddle that has no tree.

Cleaning

Brush the felt with a dandy brush, or scrub if necessary as described under washing numnahs. Keep free of hard "knots" of felt. Beware of moth damage and worn stitching. Clean the metal and leather work as in all other cases.

FIGURE 28.

A CLEAN SADDLE, PLACED ON A SADDLE HORSE, READY FOR USE

NUMNAHS

Characteristics

They are made of felt, leather, sorbo rubber, sheepskin or nylon fabric cut the shape of a saddle. They lie flat on the horse's back, and, being supple, fit any back and cause less friction than a saddle. They are attached to one of the girth tabs above the buckle by a leather loop or by an adjustable strap round the panel of the saddle above the girth tabs. Sponge or sorbo rubber squares are also used without being attached but they are clumsy and frequently brightly coloured and should not be used other than for exercising. Sheared sheepskin or nylon sheepskin are the most satisfactory.

The numnah, other than leather, when worn, depresses to about half an inch thick and has as its objects the rectifying of a badly stuffed or ill fitting saddle, or protection of the unfit horse's back when ridden for excessively long periods. It is also used by some people when show jumping and in horse trials to ensure that the horse's spine when rounded over a large fence does not contact the gullet of the saddle. If used to rectify a faulty saddle it must be regarded solely as an emergency help and the saddle should be re-stuffed or replaced by one that fits the horse. When clipping, the numnah serves as a useful guide when a saddle mark is to be left. The felt numnah can, in the case of a sore back, be cut to leave a hole over the sore spot.

Fitting

The numnah should be just slightly larger than the saddle so that when in place it is visible for about one inch all round the saddle.

Great care must be taken, especially with the leather numnah, that excessive pressure is not borne on the wither or spine. Before tightening the girths the front of the numnah should be pulled up into the front arch of the saddle.

Cleaning

Felt and all types of sheepskin—dry and brush hard with a dandy brush. Scrub if necessary, using pure soap or animal wash such as Dermoline. Air well and guard against moth.

Sponge or rubber—wash with pure soap or animal wash. Detergents should not be used for any pony furniture (clothing).

Leather—if in everyday use clean as for all other leather. When storing, cover well with vegetable oil and soften with oil again before use.

WITHER PAD

A piece of woollen or cloth material, used to place between the pommel of the saddle and the horse's wither, where the front arch of the saddle presses on the wither, or is too wide for the horse.

A wither pad may be formed by folding a stable rubber. Remember that it is an emergency aid, and that the saddle should be re-stuffed so as to fit properly, or changed, if a wither pad is necessary.

Let the saddler see the saddle on the horse to see if the saddle can be adjusted by stuffing, or, if this is not possible, take a pattern of the horse's back and send it to the saddler with the saddle (*see page 94—fitting a saddle*).

GIRTHS

Characteristics

Web. Leather. String. Nylon.

Web girths do not wear well and are liable to snap without due warning.

The practice of using a single web girth is dangerous and therefore two should always be used.

Leather girths are good. There are many types of straight, shaped and cross over leather girths. The most popular is a three fold because it is easiest to keep clean and soft. A strip of well oiled flannel or blanket should be kept in the fold to keep it soft.

String girths—good general purpose girths, which are easy to keep clean but after washing they do temporarily shrink. They let the air through and so help to prevent galling. They are less likely to slip on an unclipped pony than other kinds. They last longer than web but not so long as leather.

Nylon girths are similar to string, but tend to slip more. New nylon girths stretch when first used. Coloured ones do not look good.

Fitting

When drawn up for first mounting, there should be at least two spare holes above the buckle on each side.

Cleaning

Web, String and Nylon. Brush daily. Wash occasionally, but not too often, with pure soap and very weak ammonia or animal wash. Avoid using detergents, strong chemicals or bleach. Rinse well and never use pipe clay or whitening.

Leather. Wash, dry and soap in the same way as the saddle. Clean the buckles. Oil the inside of three-fold leather girths occasionally to keep the leather supple. Use neatsfoot oil, castor oil or dubbin. Mineral oil (i.e. motor or bicycle oil) should not be used.

STIRRUP IRONS

Characteristics

Irons should be of best quality metal. Steel is the safest and hand-forged stainless steel the most satisfactory. Plated metal chips and flakes off. Pure nickel is not advisable because it is soft and can bend. Rubber stirrup treads are sometimes used which helps to prevent the rider's foot slipping on irons that have become smooth, and they keep the rider's feet warmer and drier in winter.

Fitting

The stirrup iron should be large enough to allow half an inch at each side of the rider's foot, measured at the widest place of the boot or shoe (which should have a heel). This avoids the risk of the rider's foot becoming jammed. It is dangerous for small children to use adult stirrup irons which allow their whole foot to slip through.

Cleaning

Remove rubber treads. Wash and dry thoroughly. Clean all metals, except plain steel, with metal polish or impregnated metal polish wool and shine with a dry rubber.

Clean plain steel with metal polish and silver sand (mixed in a tin lid). Shine with a dry rubber.

Burnish with a burnisher.

All clean steel should be held in a rubber as the damp of the hand will dull it. Never let the burnisher get damp.

Safety stirrups

The kind in most general use are metal with a rubber band at one side. They should be worn with the rubber band on the outside. Unless this is done they are inclined to make the rider turn the ankle inwards.

It is essential to use these with a saddle that is fitted with a "D", instead of a stirrup bar, because the stirrup leather cannot come off in an emergency.

The disadvantages of these stirrups are:—

(1) They do not hang straight due to being weighted more on one side than the other.

(2) The inconvenience caused, when the rubber band comes undone or breaks.

The fitting and cleaning is the same as for other stirrups.

Wash and dry the rubber but do not put near heat.

BRIDLES

Parts of a snaffle bridle (*see figure 29—snaffle bridle parts ready to assemble*)

(1) The head-piece and throat lash (or latch) made on the same piece of leather.

(2) The brow band.

(3) The cheek-pieces, attached at one end to the bit and at the other end to the head-piece.

(4) The cavesson noseband on its own head-piece—which lies under the head-piece, both being threaded through both ends of the browband. Other nosebands, not shown, such as dropped, grackle and kineton, are put together in the same way.

(5) The bit (the types of which are discussed in Part I) is attached to the cheek-pieces and reins by stitches or by studs or buckles if it is required that they be detachable from the bit.

A stitched "mount" looks best.

A studded "mount" is useful for exercising and work at home as different bits and sizes of bits can be attached as required. It facilitates cleaning. A buckled "mount" is clumsy and not a good mount.

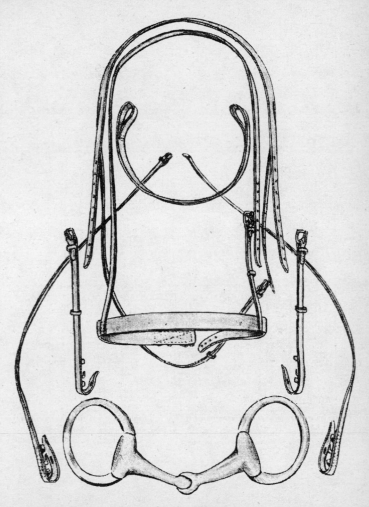

FIGURE 29. PARTS OF A SNAFFLE BRIDLE, READY TO ASSEMBLE

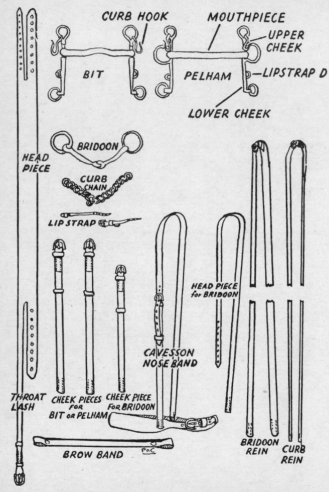

FIGURE 30.　THE PARTS OF A DOUBLE BRIDLE
(Showing also a Pelham Bit)

(6) Reins can be plain, plaited or laced leather with a centre buckle and when single are wider than those used for a double bridle. Plaited or laced reins do not slip in wet weather but are expensive and more difficult to clean. Rubber grip covered leather is used by racing riders. Linen and nylon are used by some show jumpers but neither are recommended for practical use. All reins can be attached to the bit in the same way as are the cheek-pieces.

Parts of Double and Pelham bridles

(1) The head-piece and throat lash.

(2) The brow band.

(3) The bit cheek-pieces. The bridoon head-piece and cheek-piece, which is shorter than the bit cheek-pieces. This is only used for the double bridle.

(4) The cavesson noseband.

(5) The bits are—the snaffle, called the bridoon (a fairly thin mouth-piece snaffle which can have either ring or eggbutt cheeks); and a bit or curb, the mouthpiece of which is a movable weymouth or is fixed at each end to the cheeks. The leather cheek-piece of the bridle is attached to the upper cheek-ring, and the bit rein is attached to the lower cheek ring.

A pelham bit has cheeks with three rings. The leather cheek-piece is attached to the upper ring, the snaffle rein to the ring at the end of the mouthpiece and the curb rein to the bottom ring.

Good bits are expensive but wear well. The best are made of hand-forged stainless steel. Plain steel is difficult to keep clean and plated steel chips off. Nickel, which has a yellow appearance, wears at any joint producing a sharp edge and it is also liable to bend or break.

(6) The lip strap is made in two parts each of which is attached to the D on the cheek of the bit.

(7) The curb chain is attached to the hook of each of the upper rings of the bit or pelham. It has a special link through which the lip strap is threaded.

Fitting a bridle

The following points require attention when buying or fitting a bridle. Standard bits and bridles are made in pony, cob and full sizes. As a rough guide, a pony size is suitable for up to 13.1 hh., cob size up to 15 hh., and full size for large horses. The size of the pony does not always govern the size of its head—some small ponies with large heads require cob size bits and bridles, a common type of horse requires a full size, but the thoroughbred horse only requires a cob size.

(*a*) (*See figure* 31). *The throat lash* should never be tight. Its purpose is to prevent the bridle from slipping over the pony's head.

A tight throat lash will interfere with the pony's breathing and flexing.

It should be done up to allow the full width of an adult's hand between it and the side of the jaw bone.

(*b*) *The brow band* should lie evenly below the ears without touching them, and be of such a length that it does not interfere with the hang of the head-piece. Its purpose is to prevent the head-piece from slipping back.

(*c*) *The cavesson nose-band* should be loose enough to allow the pony to open his mouth and flex his jaw. It should lie half-way between the projecting cheek-bone and the corners of the mouth and admit two fingers' breadth between the nose-band and the front of the face. Its main use is that it provides something other than the bit, to which a martingale, or lead rein, may be attached.

(*d*) *The dropped nose-band* must be very carefully fitted so that the front is well above the nostrils and the back is in the chin groove. The front should not be too wide and should remain high. This can be done by it being sewn onto a spiked ring or by a union of leather to the cheek piece (see figure 32). The cheek pieces should lie in front of a line from the pony's lips. It should be adjusted so that it is tight enough to prevent the pony from crossing his jaw or opening his mouth wide, but not so tight that it prevents the flexing of the jaw. (See figure 32: Snaffle bridle and dropped nose-band correctly fitted.)

(*e*) *The bridoon and bit* should be the correct height in the mouth. They must not be so high that they wrinkle the lips, nor so low that they touch the teeth. They should be the correct width for the mouth, sufficiently wide so as not to pinch and not so wide that they might bruise the corners of the mouth, when moving from side to side. In a double bridle the bridoon should be above the bit. (See figure 31: Double bridle put up and correctly fitted).

(*f*) *The curb chain* should be made to lie flat in the chin groove by attaching one end to the offside hook, then from the near side, twisting the chain to the right until it is flat with the loose ring in the centre hanging down. Place the base of the end link on the near-side hook with the thumb uppermost, and then the link needed for the correct fitting with the thumb underneath.

The curb chain should come into action when the cheeks of the bit are drawn back to approximately 45 degrees to the mouth.

(*g*) *The lip strap* need not be tight but must pass through the centre loose ring on the curb chain. Its uses are to hold the chain if it becomes unhooked, to prevent the cheeks of a Banbury-action bit revolving forward and up, and to prevent a horse catching hold of the cheeks of the bit.

Note. In a Banbury bit the cheeks are not fixed and can revolve round the mouth-piece.

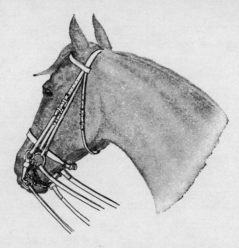

FIGURE 31.   A DOUBLE BRIDLE, CORRECTLY FITTED

Finally, run the fingers under all the head-pieces to be sure that they are not twisted and that the mane is flat, the forelock lying over the brow band. To alter the nose-band head-piece ease it up at the poll and then ease it down the other side. Do not try to pull it all from one side and so pull the bridle crooked. Stand in front to see if everything is straight and that the bit, or bits, are level in the pony's mouth. See that all keepers and runners are firm and that there are no flapping ends which look very untidy.

Cleaning

(*a*) *Preparing*. Hang up the bridle on the cleaning bracket, see figure 27 and description on page 89. Take off the nose-band, let out the cheek-pieces to the lowest hole—if the bridle is fitted for one horse note the holes which have been used. It is a good practice to take the bridle apart at least once a week. This gives an

FIGURE 32.

A SNAFFLE BRIDLE WITH DROPPED NOSEBAND, CORRECTLY FITTED

opportunity to look over all the stitching. If it has a studded mount undo it by pushing with the pad at the base of the thumb. When the stud fastening is released then the mount will be easily pulled out of the keepers. Always push any difficult buckle fastening back through the buckle from above. It is easier to undo this way than by pulling the end.

(b) *Washing.* Take the bridle off the bracket. Wash the bit with a piece of towelling in a plastic bucket using tepid water. Be careful not to let any leather part fall in the water. Examine the bit when drying to see that it has not become rough. Wash the top of the headpiece and replace on the bracket. Now the rest of the bridle can be washed keeping it taut by holding with one hand and washing with the other. When dealing with the reins step backwards away from the hooks. Wash the reins down towards the buckle and then hang them on another hook. Wash the nose-band. Now dry all leather with a chamois leather.

(c) *Preserving.* Polish bits and buckles as described for irons on page 103. Soap all leather work, putting as much on the underside as on the top. To do this the sponge can be wrapped round the straps and rubbed up and down. The sponge must not be too wet, or it would make the soap lather. If the bridle requires to be oiled, take it apart, removing the bit if possible. Oil each part well and put up with the straps in the runners only.

Put the snaffle bridle together (see figure 34). Thread the head-piece and nose-band through the brow band and hang on the hook. Assemble as if you were facing the pony. Make sure the throat lash is hanging behind and do up the cavesson head-piece. Attach the cheek-pieces. Replace all buckles back in their correct holes with the strap ends in their "keepers" and "runners". "Keepers" are stitched loops. "Runners" are loops that slide up and down. If the bridle is likely to need readjustment when next used, put the straps through the runners only and not through the keepers. If the bit was removed—replace—taking care that it is now bent out from the nutcracker joint when hanging up and the reins attached behind the cheek-pieces. A stud fastening cheek-piece is easily put together if put through both keepers and then slid back over the stud.

Put the double bridle together. Thread the head-piece through the brow band and thread the bridoon head-piece from the other side of the brow band. Then thread the cavesson from the same end as the head-piece and hang it up. After attaching the cavesson and other cheek-pieces, there will be two buckles on each side. The bridoon should lie above the bit with the bridoon reins behind the bit. Replace the lip strap.

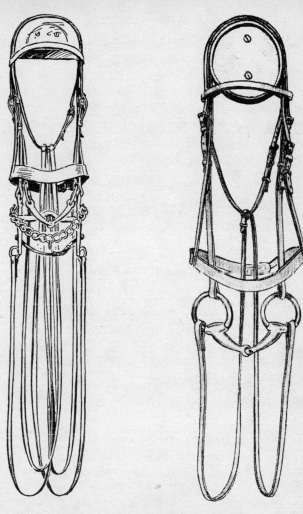

FIGURE 33. A DOUBLE BRIDLE "PUT UP"
FIGURE 34. A SNAFFLE BRIDLE "PUT UP"

Putting up

"Put Up" the snaffle bridle (see figure 34) with the reins through the throat lash and the nose-band outside the cheek-pieces. Do not buckle the nose-band, just put the end of the strap through the keeper and runner. Hang the bridle on a bridle hanger to keep the head-piece the correct shape. If you have no hanger, an empty saddle soap tin nailed to the wall makes a suitable one.

"Put Up" double bridle (see figure 33) in the same way as the snaffle bridle. Make sure that the reins are not twisted. Hang the bridle up and hook on the curb chain in front of the bit.

Remember that tack will be safer, more comfortable to use, and will last longer if kept clean and well cared for.

BREAST PLATE

Characteristics

A neck strap attached to the front "D's" of the saddle, on each side of the wither, and to the girth between the forelegs. Its useful purpose is to prevent the saddle slipping back, which may easily happen when a grass-fed pony has done some work, or on any pony which runs up light underneath.

Fitting

The neck strap should admit the width of a hand at the withers. The straps joined to the girth and "D" should be flat, without strain, when the neck strap is in its proper position.

Cleaning

The procedure is the same as for all other metal and leather.

NECK STRAP

Characteristics and uses

This article of saddlery, seldom referred to in books, is most advantageous to young riders who ride for long hours in rough undulating country, on ponies without manes and also for a pony or rider learning to jump. In a hilly, trappy country it is almost essential. The neck strap of a martingale is suitable, but in order to prevent it slipping forward when the pony lowers its head, it can have an attachment of a leather loop to the girth between the forelegs, or to the "D's" on the front arch of the saddle.

PUTTING ON A SADDLE

1. Tie up the pony before collecting your tack and keep him tied up until you have finished putting on your saddle.

Reasons. You save time. It stops him drifting, treading on your toe, or nipping and kicking other ponies. It prevents you losing him. If you do have to leave him for anything, then it stops him rolling with his saddle on and damaging the saddle. It is right to tie up your pony when you saddle up.

2. Go to the saddle room or wherever you keep your tack. Make sure before leaving that you have the saddle (*see figure* 28, *page* 99) with irons and leathers on, irons run up, the girth attached to the girth tabs on the off-side. If a numnah is used place it on the saddle horse and put the saddle on top pulling the numnah well up into the front arch. Do up the straps, or loop, round the girth tabs. Now attach the girth on the off side. Next collect a martingale if used, the bridle complete and a stick. If it is not the pony's usual bridle, adjust it so that all parts are certain to be big enough to go on the pony. Have the cheek-pieces buckled but not in their keepers and runners. Undo the back of

the nose-band and the throat lash and release the reins so that they may be carried, at the buckle, together with the top of the head-piece. If it is a double bridle unhook the curb chain on the near side, undo the lip strap and nose-band. All this is easier and quicker to do before going near the pony. It saves you running about and things being dropped or mislaid.

3. How to carry it all. See page 94.

4. It is usual to put the martingale on first, then the saddle, then the bridle. *Reasons*. The saddle settles into the pony's back and in winter warms up. It helps to prevent him blowing himself out or nipping you; both habits you will give him if he is continually saddled and girthed up all in one.

5. When you get to the pony, hang up the bridle tidily on a nearby peg, door or fence post. Do not dump it in a heap on the ground. Stand the saddle down on the front arch.

If uncertain of the pony, saddle up on the near side; otherwise make a habit of being able to do it from either side. Always keep near the pony's shoulder, where you are out of the zone of kick and are less likely to be nipped.

6. Put on the martingale with the neck strap buckle on the near side of the neck. For fitting, see page 18.

If the pony is rugged-up, see details on page 145.

7. With your hands smooth the coat where the saddle and girth will go. Be sure all the hairs are lying flat and there is no mud which would cause a sore.

8. (*a*) Pick up the saddle and with the front arch in the crook of your left arm and your right hand on the cantle, place the saddle lightly but firmly well forward on the withers.

(*b*) Slide it well back into such a position that you will not be sitting right on the pony's shoulders. Most saddles are put on too far forward.

(*c*) See that the sweat flap is down and that all is flat and smooth under the saddle-flap—if a numnah is used see that it is lying flat and pulled well up into the front arch. It should be visible for about one inch all round.

(*d*) Go quickly but quietly round in front or under the pony's neck to the off-side. See that all is flat and smooth under this flap. Let down the girths. It is *very important* to go round to do this. You cannot see by leaning over the top of the saddle and hoping you have everything flat.

(*e*) Go back to the near side, and keeping your left shoulder close to the pony's near shoulder, bend down and take hold of the girth, put through the martingale and buckle up so that the girth is not too tight but holds the saddle firmly with no fear of it slipping back. A rough guide is to be able to insert the flat of your hand. Be sure you have no skin pinched behind the elbows.

(*f*) See that the girth buckles are level and that you have at least three holes on each side to take up. You then have a correctly fitted girth—leave the buckle guards up above the buckles until the girths are finally tightened.

The Crupper (if used) must be put on when the girth is loose or before doing up the girth. Standing close to the near-hind leg, gather up the tail in the right hand and pass it through the crupper, taking care to see it is well up to the top of the tail and that all the hairs are out and lying flat. Adjust the length so that it steadies the saddle but is not so short that the tail is pulled up.

PUTTING ON A BRIDLE

For Fitting, see pages 108 to 110.

You cannot put on a bridle standing in one place all the time. Nor can you put it on when the pony has his head low or is eating.

Method 1

1. (*a*) Taking the bridle from where you hung it up, put your left hand under the brow band and head-piece, with the brow band nearest your elbow.

(*b*) Place the buckles of the reins in front of the head-piece on your left forearm. You now have both hands free.

2. Untie the pony's head rope.

3. Place the reins over the pony's head and neck. You now have an anchor when you remove the halter.

4. Hang the halter or head collar where the pony was tied up. Do not just drop it where you and the pony may tread on it. If in a box or stable, turn the pony round to the light.

5. (*a*) With your right hand take hold of the headpiece of the bridle.

(*b*) Slide your left hand under the pony's muzzle letting the mouthpiece of the bit rest on your first finger and thumb.

(*c*) Bend your first finger and feel between the pony's lips (on the off-side) where there is a gap between the teeth. This makes him open his mouth.

(*d*) Keeping your right hand close to his forehead, draw up the bridle, using your left hand to guide the bit into the pony's mouth.

(*e*) The left hand can now assist the right hand to pass the head-piece over each ear in turn. Take care to smooth the mane and forelock and run your finger round under the head-piece to see that nothing is twisted.

It is easy to remember the order for doing up the various buckles because you start at the ears and work down.

Be sure that as you do up each strap you put the end neatly through its keeper and runner.

6. (*a*) Do up the throat lash to admit the full width of your hand between it and the side of the jaw bone.

(*b*) Stand in front and see the brow band is level, just below the ears but not touching them. See that the bridle is on straight.

(*c*) See the nose-band is inside (i.e. next to the nose all round); put on the standing martingale (if used), buckle the nose-band so that two fingers can be inserted between it and the front of the face. Adjust the length on the near side. Ease up or down at the head-piece to straighten. Do not pull it through both loops of the brow band at once (it is hard work and you only pull your bridle crooked).

(*d*) Adjust the bit on both sides, counting the holes to make sure it is level. Adjust the bridoon on the off-side, easing it up or down at the headpiece.

(*e*) Standing on the near side, twist the curb chain towards the pony's body until it is flat and hook it on to the end link. Always keep the end links hooked on even if you shorten the curb chain. Never allow them to dangle (see page 109 for fitting).

(*f*) Pass the strap end of the lip strap through the loose ring on the curb chain and buckle it.

7. Check the martingale fitting (see page 18). If using a running martingale, adjust it on the bit reins.

8. Finally, pick out the pony's feet (if you have been working in a box or stable). Collect your stick and when you are outside look round to see that the saddlery is correct and comfortable.

Remember, "stirrups up means girths loose", as they should now be. For the next stage see "Mounting" (page 1).

If you leave a pony saddled and bridled, always put the ends of the reins under the stirrups to prevent him putting his head down and treading on the reins or rolling. Alternatively replace the halter or head collar over the bridle and tie up the pony.

Putting on a bridle (method 2)

1 to 4. Same as for method 1.

5. (a) Put your right hand *under* the pony's jaw and up round the other side to the centre of his face, just above his nostrils.

(b) Then take both cheek-pieces in this hand. Keep it close to the pony's face.

(c) Your left hand opens his mouth and guides in the bit, as in method 1.

(d) Your right hand eases the bridle up. Then, using both hands, place the headpiece over the pony's ears.

Continue from 5 (e) as in method 1.

With method 2 you are closer to the pony. You have your right hand to steady his head and stop it moving sideways, upwards or downwards. Therefore you have more control.

OFF-SADDLING FROM EITHER SIDE

You usually off-saddle in this order: saddle, bridle, then martingale.

If it is raining try to off-saddle under cover so as not to get the lining of the saddle wet. When you dismount run up your irons and loosen the girths.

Before you take off your saddle:—

(*a*) Take the reins over the pony's head and slip the ends on to the arm nearest his head.

(*b*) Raise the flap and undo the girths, letting them go gently.

(*c*) Slip off the martingale loop from the girth.

(*d*) With one hand on the front arch and the other hand on the cantle, slide the saddle off towards you and on to your forearm with the front arch in the crook of your elbow. Take hold of the girths with the other hand as they come over the back. Place their greasy, not muddy, side on the seat of the saddle (grease washes off, but mud scratches).

(*e*) Stand the saddle down carefully and safely—not too near the pony.

(*f*) Run your hands over the pony's back and girth groove to feel for lumps or soreness. Then pat briskly, not heavily, to dry and restore circulation. Do not forget that a pony has *two* sides to be dealt with.

TAKING OFF A BRIDLE

1.   Have a halter or head collar near and ready to put on, or put your arm through it and hang it on your shoulder out of the way.

2.   Put the reins back over the pony's neck (you had the ends on your arm to off-saddle). You now have something to control the pony if he moves.

3.   (a) Standing on the near side, unhook the curb chain on the near side. Leave the lip strap done up; it will not get caught up or interfere, and it prevents the curb chain from getting lost if you have to carry the bridle far.

(b) Undo the nose-band and slip off the end of the standing martingale.

(c) Undo the throat lash.

You now have everything undone and safe for taking it off the pony's head.

4.   (a) Place your left hand on the pony's face, well above the nostrils.

(b) With your right hand slip the head-piece over the ears and slowly place it on your left forearm.

Important. Allow the pony to ease the bit out of his mouth slowly. If it is dropped out quickly he may throw up his head, get caught up with the bit and hurt his mouth. He may remember and be difficult next time. For the same reason *never* take off a bridle with the curb chain hooked up.

(c) Slip off the martingale neckstrap and slide it, together with the bridle headpiece, but not the reins, up to your left shoulder. You now have both hands free to put on the halter or head collar.

5.   Then take the reins over the pony's head and on to your left shoulder and tie up the pony. Look at both corners of his mouth in case his bit has rubbed. Look inside his mouth to see that the bit has not injured the bars or the inside of his cheeks. Pull his ears if they are damp or cold.

6.   Keeping the bridle and martingale on the left shoulder, pick up the saddle, and girth, and your stick and carry them correctly (see page 94) to a place of safety. Put the saddle on the peg or saddle horse. Hang the bridle and martingale on the cleaning bracket hooks.

In this way you will leave nothing behind, nor will you trail the girth or reins on the ground.

SADDLING AND OFF-SADDLING A RUGGED-UP PONY

Saddling up

Proceed as far as detail 6 on page 116, then undo the roller and put it neatly on the manger.

Undo the breast strap and fold the front of the rug back over the pony's loins.

Put on the saddle and do up the girths. Draw the front of the rug forward over the saddle. Do not buckle the breast strap because if the rug slips (as it may do with no roller to hold it) it will then drop right off and not get caught round the pony's neck.

Finally, before leading the pony out of the box, strip off the rug, fold it neatly and put it on the manger or over the box door, if under cover.

Off-saddling

Off-saddle as on page 121, then put on the rug and roller and do up the breast strap (see pages 144 and 145 for method).

PART III.

HORSEMASTERSHIP

EVERY good horseman will wish also to be a good horse-master.

The chance of succeeding today is better than ever before because of the vast wealth of experience inherited, and because the decrease in professional grooms has led to the rise of the owner-groom.

In dealing with horses there is a right and a wrong way of doing everything. Sometimes there are several right ways of doing the same thing. The man who does things the right way is said to possess horse sense. If he does it instinctively he is said to be born with horse sense. For the remainder, the art is acquired by a process of study and experience. Sometimes the experience is painful, as when a kick is suffered or the loss of a favourite pony results from some wrong act.

In general, the "right" way in which to do anything with a horse is the "safe" way—safe to the groom and free from danger to the animal. It is not always possible to know the right way unless it is first demonstrated or taught. To teach a right way in all things is the object of the Pony Club.

HORSEMASTERSHIP AND STABLEMANAGEMENT

This section of the book covers the entire care of horses and ponies under all conditions throughout the 365 days of the year, whether they be kept at grass or stabled.

Horses and ponies may be required for hunting, hacking, horse trials and horse events, gymkhanas, polo, being driven or used for breeding. Consequently it is necessary to have the knowledge and ability to deal with a wide variety of problems which comprise the following: handling; stable routine; watering; feeding; forage; grazing; exercise; conditioning; grooming; clothing; clipping; trimming; turning out correctly; travelling; shoeing; conformation; minor ailments; nursing a sick or injured horse; breeds and types of ponies and the fitting and care of saddlery.

HANDLING PONIES*

Understanding of, and sympathy with, a horse's mentality, is essential to success. A horse is very much a creature of habit and favours the same thing being done in the same way and at the same time every day. Picking out feet, for example, is much more easily accomplished if carried out in the same rotation each time it is done. A pony brought into a stable from grass each night is more easily dealt with if the operation is carried out at the same hour each evening. It is a good plan, therefore, to adopt and adhere to a fixed daily stable routine.

It is necessary to appreciate that the gregarious instinct in horses is highly developed. They love the company of their own kind. Much that might otherwise prove difficult can often be accomplished easily by keeping stable companions within sight or hearing of one another.

For the rest, the golden rules are: speak quietly; handle gently; avoid sudden movements; habits that everyone charged with the care of ponies must possess or acquire. There is simply no place in the stable for the rough, loud-voiced groom.

Speaking

Speak before approaching; speak before handling; speak before moving. This is a simple but most important lesson to learn.

---

*NOTE: This section is also available as a film for teaching purposes viz. The Pony Club Instructional Film, "Horse Sense".

Repetition of a spoken word will soon become recognised and a horse or pony learns much, too, from the inflection of the voice and the tone and manner in which the words are used and soon knows the voice of the one who feeds him or from whom some kindness is to be expected. For safety sake, *speak*.

The approach

The approach should always be to the shoulder, whether the horse be in a field or stable. Approach in the direction of the shoulder and speak. When near enough pat or stroke the lower neck or shoulder.

To fit a halter

Loosen the nose-band and pass the free end of the rope over the neck to secure the animal. Then manoeuvre the nose-band over the muzzle and finally the head-piece over the ears. A knot is then placed on the leading side to prevent the nose-band becoming too loose or too tight (see figure 35).

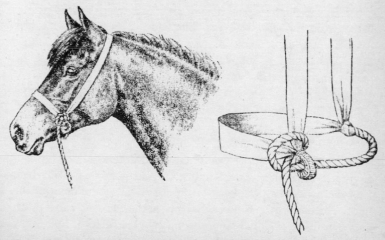

FIGURE 35. A HALTER CORRECTLY FITTED

To lead in hand

With a strange animal work from the near-side, since most will expect to be led from the near-side. The right hand is placed on the rope or reins, back of the hand upwards, a short distance from the headstall or bridle. Do not weigh on the rope or reins. The slack of the rope or reins is gathered up in the left hand. When leading from the off-side, reverse the position of the hands. It is good to accustom a horse or pony to be led from either side.

To move the animal, speak and walk forward. A trained horse or pony will readily follow. Most refuse to move if stared in the face.

In turning check the pace and then move the animal round by pushing the head away from you because he then keeps his head up, his hocks under him and remains balanced.

Handling the legs

To lift the foreleg speak first of all. Then place a hand on the neck and turn to face the tail. The hand is then run down over the shoulder, elbow, back of the knee and tendons. On reaching the fetlock say "Up" and squeeze the joint. Catch the toe of the foot with the fingers of the other hand and hold it. Less weight falls on the arm if the foot is held at the toe rather than by grasping the pastern. If he declines to lift his foot when spoken to he may be induced to do so by leaning against the shoulder and so pushing his weight across on to the other limb.

For the hind leg speak again and stand abreast of the hip and face backwards, placing the hand nearest the pony on the quarters. Run the hand down the back of the leg as far as the point of the hock. Then move the hand to the front of the hock and run it down on the inside front of the cannon bone. On reaching the fetlock say "Up", move the joint slightly backwards when the pony raises the foot and then slide the hand down to encircle the hoof from the inside. Do not lift high and do not carry far back, both of which will probably be resisted since they upset the pony's balance (see figure 36).

FIGURE 36. PICKING UP A HIND LEG

THE STABLED HORSE AND PONY

Our knowledge of the care and management of the stabled horse is a legacy from the era when it was an essential condition of life that horses should be available immediately when required. To go out and catch a wet and muddy horse at grass every time a carriage was ordered would have been unworkable. Hence the solution which stabling provided.

It is to be remembered, too, that this was also the era of wealth, leisure, ample labour and extravagant dress. This was reflected in the stables where it was a special pride to turn out horses, carriages and their attendant staff at the highest possible level of cleanliness and smartness. Though much has necessarily been lost in the intervening years, the tradition of cleanliness and smart appearance where horses are concerned is still with us today. It should be the ambition, therefore, of every good horseman to strive for the highest attainable alike in the turn-out of horses, standards of stable management, care of tack and cleanliness of the stable premises, and so to carry on the tradition of our great inheritance.

CONSTRUCTION OF STABLES

Loose boxes

Are greatly to be preferred in that the horse is allowed a greater measure of freedom, greater comfort and is encouraged to lie down and rest. Boxes need to be about 14 ft. by 12 ft. to accommodate a hunter, and 12 ft. by 10 ft. to accommodate a pony.

Access to loose boxes is either by way of a stable door direct from the yard or by a stable door and passage-way within the stable. In the former case the door ought to be in two parts so that the upper portion can be hooked back and left open so permitting the horse to look over the lower portion at will. Horses greatly appreciate the chance to view what is taking place in their immediate neighbourhood. Grilles are sometimes provided for fastening across the open top half of the door. Such prevent a horse jumping out, biting at passersby, loosening the top bolt and check weaving (*see figure* 37).

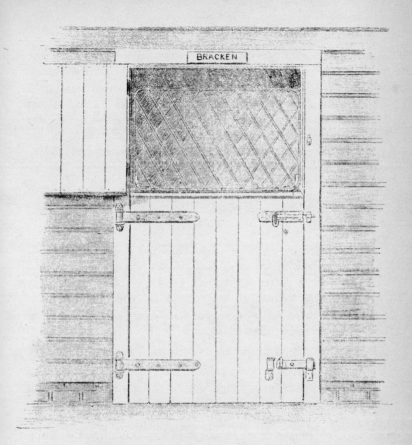

FIGURE 37.   TO SHOW GRILLE ACROSS TOP HALF OF DOOR
Double bolts to lower door, viz.
Bolt at top.   Foot operated bolt at bottom

Doors should be four feet wide. Narrow doorways are dangerous.
It is important that the doors of loose boxes open outwards so that

access may be gained without disturbing bedding, and particularly so, should an animal become cast in his box near to the door.

Latches of such doors need to be of a special non-projecting type so that there is no risk of the horse being injured by them when passing through. Two are necessary, one at the top of the door and another at the bottom, and the lower one may with advantage be foot operated (*see figure* 37). Two latches make for greater security and the lower one prevents damage through kicking. An overhang or verandah outside a row of boxes is an advantage since it affords protection against the weather to both horse and groom.

Stalls

Have the advantage of providing for the accommodation of a greater number of animals in a given space, for an economy of labour and a saving of bedding material.

Disadvantages are that they are unable to move around and may become bored because they cannot look out; nor have they access to fresh air. A shy or nervous animal may lack rest by being bullied by the one in the adjoining stall.

Access to stalls is invariably by way of a passage within the stable.

Swinging Bail stalls (*see figure* 38). These are sometimes used in Pony Club camps and by riding schools for the temporary accommodation of ponies caught up from grass. Such are easily cleaned and permit free circulation of air and so ready drying off of the standings. Bails should be approximately the length of the stall. They must be hung sufficiently high to prevent a pony getting a leg over and it is usual to hang them slightly higher at the front end than at the back. They should be suspended with stout cord and a quick release knot. Should a pony get a leg over the bail he can then be quickly released or the cord cut by a penknife. Chains and wire should not be used. One of the great disadvantages of the swinging bail is that it affords no security against bullying and the injury occasioned by neck biting.

FIGURE 38.   USE OF SWINGING BAILS AS STALL DIVISIONS

Floors

The essentials are that the material shall be non-slippery, impervious to moisture, long-wearing and that it shall not strike cold to the horse when he lies down. Concrete meets only two of these conditions and though relatively cheap and easily obtainable is far from being satisfactory. If employed it is essential that it be given a rough facing. A good answer is the special yellow or blue stable bricks to be found in most high-class stabling.

Stable floors must necessarily slope slightly to allow for drainage, but this should be the minimum necessary for the purpose. With loose boxes drainage should preferably be towards the opposite front corner to the door with an exit hole which should be draught proof connecting with an open gulley outside. Drains running within the box just inside the door are objectionable in that they give the horse a wet standing and insecure foothold when looking out. Covered drains are difficult to keep clean.

Ventilation

This is an important matter. All experience goes to show that horses keep fitter and more free from coughs and colds when

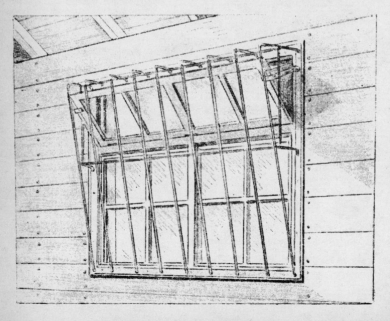

FIGURE 39.   A VENTILATION WINDOW

adequate fresh air is supplied. Warmth is to be secured by means of additional clothing rather than by way of a stuffy atmosphere.

To provide for this the simplest plan is to leave the top portion of the stable door open, day and night, summer and winter. This is almost always possible provided the stable faces south, and the bottom portion is of sufficient height to exclude draughts. A south aspect for this reason is always to be preferred. There should also be a window on the same side as the door with the glass protected by iron bars. The window may be combined with a "Sheringham" type of ventilator which opens inwards. This permits fresh air to enter in an upward direction and directs it over, and not onto the back of the horse (*see figure* 39). For greater comfort partitions between boxes ought to go right up to the roof.

Stable fittings

In practice few are necessary and the more free a box or stall is of encumbrances the better.

A ring at breast-level for tying the horse up to the manger, and others at eye-level for short-racking the horse and for the hay net must be regarded as essentials. One of the short-rack rings should be so placed that it permits the horse to feed if necessary. They need to be really firmly fitted.

Mangers at breast-level, placed either in a corner or along a wall, are to be found in most stables. They need to be shallow enough to prevent a horse getting his jaw caught in them, deep enough to prevent him throwing his food out, broad enough to prevent a horse biting them. Improvised mangers are rarely a success and invariably fail in all these essentials. Fitted mangers may also include a separate compartment for hay. Hay racks, fitted above head-level, are now generally condemned as they necessitate a horse feeding at an unnatural level, with the attendant risk of dust falling into his eyes.

Gravity, or lever-operated water bowls are favoured by some horse owners but they ought not to be sited near the manger or hay rack lest they become blocked with food.

FIGURE 40.   A PONY CORRECTLY SECURED BY LOG AND ROPE

Where fitted mangers, hayracks and water bowls are dispensed with altogether, the cleaning of the stable is greatly facilitated. Feeding is carried out at ground-level—a much more natural position—a movable galvanised iron feed tin or a wooden feed box being used for the purpose. Circular feed tins, about 18 inches in diameter, or wood boxes with sloping sides, about 15 inches high and 18 inches square at the top, meet every requirement, are long-lasting and are easily cleaned. Such should be removed when the feed is finished. Hay is fed on the ground loose or more economically, from a hay-net secured to one of the short-rack rings. Water is provided from a bucket.

Large, hinged rings half way up the wall which fold downwards when not in use are found in some stables. They are designed to take a feed or water bucket when the ring is raised and so prevent the bucket being knocked over.

Securing

Horses are secured in stables by a headstall and headrope, and for this purpose the latter is always attached to the back "D" of the nose-band. The headrope is either tied to the manger ring, or, better still, passed through the ring and secured to a log. The log is placed at the end of the rope so that it just touches the ground when the pony stands up to the manger. The advantage of the latter system is that the log takes the slack out of the rope so preventing a horse getting a leg over the rope and becoming cast (*see figure* 40). The use of a log is essential in a stall where the horse remains tied up all the time.

To short-rack a horse, tie up to the ring on the wall at eye-level. This ring is provided for use whenever it is desired to restrict a horse's movement, viz. to prevent him turning round and biting during grooming or to prevent him lying down after being groomed.

To place a horse on the pillar reins, turn him round in his stall and fasten the reins or chains which hang on the heel posts to the side "D's" of his headstall. Pillar reins have various uses, but, in particular, they are used to keep a saddled or bridled animal under control until he is required to turn out.

In tying up a horse it is most important that some recognised form of quick-release knot be employed. A simple and efficient form of such is shown in figure 41.

Neck straps are sometimes used for securing ponies but they are much inferior to headstalls except in cases where a pony has developed the habit of slipping his headstall. They are sometimes

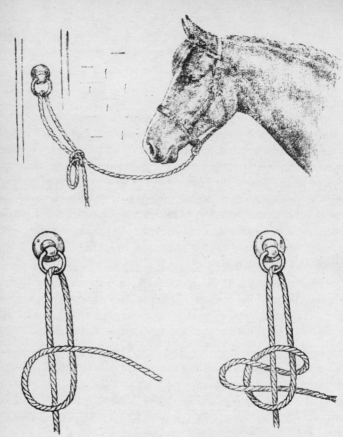

FIGURE 41.   A QUICK RELEASE KNOT

employed in the stall stables of riding schools for the temporary control of ponies brought in from grass and then have the great advantage that they permit the bridle to be fitted without releasing the pony.

Electric Light Switches. These ought always to be placed outside the stable and never within, and in a position where the animal cannot interfere with them. They should be of a special "stable" type designed to prevent electrocution should a shod horse seize them with his teeth.

Stable utensils

A stable barrow, stable shovel, broom, stable fork with blunted points, four-prong fork, a skep for droppings, a plastic bowl or bucket for the corn feed, hay nets, stable buckets, a length of hosepipe, a sheet of material such as sackcloth or hessian for carrying straw, must be regarded as essentials.

When not actually in use, utensils must be stored outside the box or stall, so that risk of injury to the animal is avoided. They should be hung on special hooks placed high up on the wall.

BEDDING

Some form of bedding material is necessary for the stabled horse, to allow him to lie down and rest, to encourage him to stale, provide insulation, and to prevent jar to the feet during long hours spent standing on a hard surface.

Straw

On the whole, wheat straw makes the best bedding material. It is normally reasonably cheap, and readily obtainable. It is easily stored when baled, gives a bright appearance to the stable, makes a warm comfortable bed, is easily handled and permits free drainage. Finally, soiled straw bedding has a high manurial value.

Oat straw may also be used as a bedding material but being more palatable, especially the spring-grown, ponies are inclined to eat it. Barley straw is less satisfactory as the awns on the ears are prickly and irritate the skin, but barley straw from a combine harvester is often free of awns and makes good bedding.

Management of straw bedding

On first going into the stable in the morning the box should first be "mucked out", soiled portions of the bedding being separated from the clean by the use of the stable fork so that only the dung and wet portions are discarded. In doing this the dry bedding should be thrown back to the rear of the stall or box and the soiled portion put on a sheet placed at the entrance to the box or stall, so as to permit proper cleaning of the floor and for the floor to air and dry off. Later the bedding is replaced so that the horse can lie down and rest in the afternoon and does not have to stand on a bare surface. In the evening the bed is remade (i.e. bedding-down). In doing this the used straw is put down first of all and then fresh clean straw added as may prove necessary. In making the bed the straw should be well tossed if baled, but if trussed the straws should lie across each other and not all in the same direction. It is customary to bed more thickly around the four walls of a loose box or sides of a stall as an additional precaution against injury or draught. A good deep bed makes for comfort and is more economical in the long run.

Good management requires that droppings be removed as soon as passed. This is done by lifting the straw beneath and tipping into a special basket or tin made for the purpose called a "dung skep". Plastic laundry baskets are a popular substitute.

If weather permits, it is a far better plan to remove the bulk of the bedding from the stable altogether in the morning and spread it outside in the sunlight and fresh air. Such dries and deodorizes it, prolongs its life and restores its resilience.

"To judge a man's stable management, visit the manure heap". Slack lazy methods will be reflected there in a pile of only partly expended straw. A groom who handles his bedding correctly will certainly be careful and energetic in his other duties also.

A method of bedding down horses, known as the "deep litter system" is now favoured by many horse owners. Under this plan fresh straw is added daily to an existing very deep bed and only the soiled portions removed. The advantages claimed for this is a saving of labour, the provision of a deep warm bed and the daily shaking up of the bed unnecessary. Only when the bed has attained a thickness of more than 2 feet is the whole removed and a new build up started. Adequate ventilation is a necessity if the box is not to become offensive.

Shavings and sawdust, either separately or jointly, make a good clean, bright and comfortable bed for horses, and often a cheap one, too. If both are employed together then the sawdust forms the under layer.

As bedding material, shavings and sawdust require constant attention and the frequent removal of droppings.

Peat Moss is popular with many and makes an excellent bed. It is particularly valuable where risk of fire is a consideration. Wet and soiled patches must be changed frequently and the bed forked and raked over daily. In this way the peat is kept soft and sweet and does not become packed and soggy.

Peat, when first put down is apt to prove a somewhat dusty bedding. The disposal of soiled peat sometimes presents a problem.

Disposal of manure

If the manure pit is in the vicinity of the stables, arrangements must be made for it to be emptied very frequently or sold under contract. If manure is to be stacked, a place some way from the stables should be chosen and the manure stored in three heaps, viz. (1) the oldest, the well-rotted manure ready for garden use, (2) a second pile, discontinued and in the process of rotting, and (3) the pile in process of formation. Muck heaps should be close packed by beating down with the stable shovel and well squared off. This assists decomposition and the heat generated inhibits fly breeding.

CLOTHING

The following are the articles of horse clothing commonly in use:

Day rugs of woollen material bound with braid of another colour. For warmth in the stable by day. Such rugs often bear the owner's initials in the corner.

A roller to match. Used to keep the rug in position. These are padded where they rest on each side of the spine. Sometimes a felt pad is used in addition as an extra protection.

Night rugs of hemp or jute lined with check woollen material, for warmth in the stable at night. These are often provided with a webbing surcingle sewn onto them, but this may lead to pressure on the spine and is better cut off, a roller being employed instead. Night rugs are subject to considerable soiling when the pony lies down, for which reason a cheaper pattern rug than the day rug is employed.

Leather roller to keep the rug in place.

A roller pad for use under the roller, to prevent pressure on the spine.

Breast strap to prevent the roller slipping back.

Horse blankets of fawn wool used on a clipped pony beneath the rug during the colder months of the winter.

Stable bandages of wool, 4 inches wide in sets of four.

In addition, the following articles of clothing are employed in special circumstances:—

New Zealand rugs (*see figure* 42). These rugs are made of waterproof canvas partly lined with wool, and are designed for

FIGURE 42. A NEW ZEALAND RUG

use on horses and ponies at grass. They are not intended to be worn in the stable. They are provided with a surcingle sewn on in the back region, the ends of which pass through the sides of the rug. In addition leg straps are provided to fasten around the thighs and these should be linked, the one through the other where they pass under the belly as a precaution against soreness through chafing. The special merit of these rugs is that they afford an animal protection against wind and rain and do not become dislodged when he gets down and rolls. They are particularly valuable as day rugs on clipped animals turned out to grass for a few hours on a winter's day.

Horses need to be accustomed to these rugs before being turned loose in them as the stiffness of the canvas and the rub of the leg straps may upset a nervous pony the first time they are worn.

Summer sheets of cotton used to protect the groomed horse and pony against dust and the worry of flies. They ought to be provided with "fillet-strings", which hang around the quarters from side to side to prevent the sheet blowing up in the wind.

Anti-sweat rugs made of open cotton mesh are popular today for use either as sheets or coolers for an overheated horse or pony in summer time or under the night rug in place of straw in a clipped animal that is sweating or tending to "break out" on return from work in winter time.

Arched rollers provided with a metal bar connecting the two sides in the back region avoid pressure on the spine and minimise the risk of the horse getting cast when rolling in his box.

Knee-caps are used as a precaution against injury to the knees when travelling, or as a protection against the accident known as "broken knees" in valuable horses at exercise. The upper strap should be firmly fastened, the buckle on the outside of the limb, but the lower strap is fitted loosely so that flexion of the knee is not interfered with. In removing knee-caps the lower strap should be unfastened first. Similarly, **hock boots** are employed to protect the hocks when travelling. **Tail guards** are used to protect the tail in similar circumstances.

Rugging-up

The rug or sheet must first be gathered up and then thrown well forward over the horse's back. The front part is then sorted out and the buckle fastened. Now go behind the horse and pull the rug back into position using both hands. This is one of the few occasions when it is permissible to stand immediately behind a horse. Next place the roller in position to buckle up on the near side. A roller pad, if used, is placed beneath it behind the withers. Then move round to the off side and see that the roller hangs well forward, i.e. where the girth goes, otherwise it will slip forward and be loose when the horse moves. Buckle up the roller on the near side, care being taken to buckle firmly but not tightly. Smooth down the rug beneath the roller on both sides by running the fingers down between roller and rug, at the same time giving the rug a slight pull to ease it forward in front of each elbow, thus preventing a drag on the points of the shoulders. Do up the breast strap which should lie loosely above the points of the shoulders. Finally, check the pressure of the rug around the neck and shoulder. It is important to ensure that the rug fits the animal, i.e. that it is neither too large nor too small. In either case, sore withers may result apart from other discomfort caused.

If a blanket is used in addition to the rug, then it is put on first of all and in a similar manner. Care should be taken that an ample portion lies on the neck and that the back of the blanket does not extend beyond the root of the tail. The rug is then added, and after adjustment of the roller or surcingle the surplus portion of the blanket lying on the neck is folded back as an additional precaution against slipping.

Off-rugging

From the near-side unbuckle the roller or surcingle, remove, fold up and place in the corner of the box. The breast buckle of the rug is then unfastened and, with both hands, the front portion of the rug and blanket is folded back over the top of the back portion. Then, with the left hand in the centre-front, and the right hand in the centre-back, remove rug and blanket together in one gentle backward sweep in the direction of the lie of the coat. As the rugs leave the horse's back they will automatically be folded four-square and can be placed in the corner of the box while not in use.

Stable bandages

These are made of wool. In skilful hands they are very beneficial but if they are wrongly or carelessly applied they become a danger. The ringed marks on a leg or the lump on a tendon tell of a bandage put on carelessly or too tight.

Bandages have various uses besides actual warmth and comfort, viz. with straw underneath to dry off wet legs on return from work; for protection against injury; to prevent legs filling with a pony which is not at work. For all such purposes they are applied so as to cover as much of the leg as possible, from knee or hock down to the coronet. Some prefer to use cotton wool or gamgee tissue beneath stable bandages for extra warmth.

Before commencing to bandage a leg be sure that the bandage is correctly rolled. To roll a bandage properly the tapes should be neatly folded across the width of the material and then rolled with the sewn side inwards.

In bandaging a leg start just below the knee or hock, passing the bandage round the leg in even turns until the coronet is reached. Here the bandage will take a natural turn upwards. Continue unrolling in an upward direction and finish off at the starting place. The tapes should be tied so that the knot lies to the outside or the inside of the leg and not in front, where it will press on the bone, or at the back, where it will press on the tendons. It is correct to fasten the tapes in a bow and to tuck in the spare ends (*see figure* 43A).

Exercising bandages

Sometimes also called pressure or support bandages. They are made of stockinette or crepe $2\frac{1}{2}$ to 3 inches wide. This form of bandage is used at work to support the back tendons, to reinforce weak or strained tendons or to protect the leg from thorns or brambles. Actually horses rarely require exercising bandages.

They are applied with a considerable measure of firmness from just below the knee to just above the fetlock joint, but must not interfere with the action of either joint. To ensure that the bandage does not slip the following method of putting on should be adopted. Unroll about ten inches of the bandage and hold this portion obliquely across the outside of the leg and close to the knee (*see figure* 43B). The roll of the bandage should be close to the leg with the spare end held by the other hand extended beyond. Take one turn round the leg with the bandage and allow the spare end to fall over and down the outside of the leg. Unroll the bandage neatly down the leg and over the spare end. When the fetlock joint is reached, turn up the remaining few inches of the spare end and

FIGURE 43. A. STABLE BANDAGES

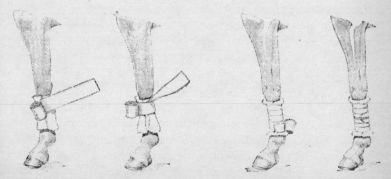

FIGURE 43. B. EXERCISING BANDAGES

continue unrolling upwards until the starting point is arrived at. Tie in the same way as for a stable bandage, or, for greater security, tie in a knot or sew on.

The use of a thick layer of cotton wool or gamgee tissue beneath exercising bandages is necessary. Such provide for better support and permits a greater measure of pressure without the risk of pressure injuries, as when a bandage becomes overtight through getting wet.

Removing bandages

Untie the tapes and unwind quickly, passing the freed parts of the bandage from hand to hand. Never roll when removing. When clear of the leg the back tendons and the fetlock should be given a brisk rub with the palms of the hands. Then hang the bandages up to air and dry.

It is dangerous to kneel in the vicinity of a horse's legs. Adopt a bending or crouching position for the purpose.

Tail bandages

Tail bandages should be made of stockinette 2½ to 3 inches wide. They are used to save the tail from injury or rubbing during travelling, to improve the appearance of the tail, and to keep the hairs of a pulled tail in position. The following rules should be observed: tail bandages should never be used to excess; they should never be left on all night and in the case of a stabled animal they should be put on after exercise and grooming and removed at evening stables.

To apply a tail bandage damp the hair first of all with a water brush. To wet the bandage is wrong as it may lead to shrinking of the material and injury to the tail, and will certainly cause the hairs of the tail to lie in the direction of the roll. Place the left hand under the tail, unroll about eight inches and place this spare piece under the tail holding the end in the left hand and the roll of the bandage in the right. Keep the left hand on the root of the tail until the spare end is secured. The first turn is often difficult to make securely but this may be overcome by making the next turn above it. Unroll the bandage round and evenly down the tail just short of the last tail bone. Tie the tapes neatly but no tighter than necessary to secure firmness. Then bend the tail back into a comfortable position (*see figure* 52).

To remove a tail bandage grasp it nearest the dock with both hands and slide off the tail in a downwards direction.

Care of clothing

Horse clothing is an expensive item of stable equipment, but with proper care can be made to last for years. Regular brushing and an occasional airing or sunning when not in use is desirable. Winter clothing not required for use in the summer should be scrubbed and, when dry, stored away, folded and packed, with moth balls, since moth is one of the commonest causes of deterioration to horse clothing. Another plan is to send winter clothing to a cleaners or to a laundry before storing away.

Fire

All animals are very fearful of fire and horses are no exception. Smoking in stables should be forbidden and peat moss litter should be employed where any risk of fire exists, as for example aboard ship.

Normally a horse terrified by fire will not face it nor leave his stable even though the doors be open.

In the event of an outbreak of fire proceed as follows: Cut the horse loose if tied up; remove jacket and throw over the horse's head, ears in sleeve holes. Then lead out of the stable. Place the horse in a current of air since horses suffer dangerously from the inhalation of smoke. In severe cases a veterinary surgeon should be sent for without delay.

A PROGRAMME OF STABLE ROUTINE

The following specimen programme is intended to serve as a guide to the manner in which the various stable duties may be fitted into the day's work and to show the hour at which each is best performed. It includes a plan for four feeds in the course of the day.

Considerable adjustment will, of course, be necessary to meet varying conditions and individual cases.

The care of the hunter on a hunting day, and the care of a grass-kept pony on a hunting day, or the day of a Pony Club rally is dealt with on pages 214 to 220.

6.30 a.m.   Stables.
               Look round the pony to see that he has suffered no
                  injury during the night.
               Put on headstall.
               Adjust rugs.
               Water the pony.
               Tie up a small net of hay.
               Muck out.
               Pick out feet.
               Throw up rugs and quarter.
               Replace rugs.

7.30 a.m.   FIRST FEED.

9.00 a.m.   Remove droppings.
              Remove clothing.
              Saddle up.
              Exercise.
              On return remove bridle and saddle.
              Allow the pony to stale and roll.
              Water.

11.30 a.m.   Rack up.
              Groom.
              Put on day rugs.
              Refill water bucket.
              Un-rack.
              SECOND FEED.
              Tie up a full net of hay.
              Set fair stable and yard.

4.00 p.m.   Rack up.
              Remove droppings.
              Pick out feet.
              Shake up bedding.
              Remove day rug.
              Rug up with night rug.
              Fill water bucket.
              Remove headstall.

4.30 p.m.   THIRD FEED.
              Clean saddlery.

7.00 p.m.   Remove droppings.
              Shake up bedding.
              Refill water bucket.
              Tie up a full net of hay
              FOURTH FEED.

THE GRASS-KEPT PONY*

ADVANTAGES AND DISADVANTAGES OF KEEPING AT GRASS

Advantages

A natural system in consequence of which ponies keep fitter, healthier and happier. Far less attention is required, thus a corresponding saving of time and wages. Ponies exercise themselves. The system of feeding is nearer to nature as grass, the natural food, becomes the mainstay and the ponies eat when and how they like. There is less risk of injury to wind and limb compared with the stabled horse since the legs and lungs, being constantly in use, are much more ready to withstand the demands which work makes upon them.

Disadvantages

Ponies are not always available when required, and may be very wet. In some cases the field is at a distance from the house and in other cases the pony refuses to be caught. If land is not available at home there may be real difficulty in finding fields which can be rented, or a farmer who is willing and able to accept a pony for grazing.

GENERAL MANAGEMENT

A pony kept at grass should be seen frequently. The pony ought to be caught up and handled daily in order to ensure that it has suffered no injury, and also to facilitate the catching up of the pony when required for work.

---

*NOTE: This subject is dealt with in greater detail in the Pony Club Publication "Keeping a Pony at Grass".

The occasion for catching up a pony ought also to be that for feeding, but if regular feeding is not being practised, then in place thereof some reward should be offered, such as a few oats or pony cubes, a slice of apple or even a piece of bread. If this procedure is carried out at the same hour each day and includes a set "call" to the pony, the great majority of ponies will respond and so come easily to hand when required.

A reward offered in this way should be fed from a feed tin or bucket and not direct from the pocket, a procedure which sometimes leads a pony to become a confirmed biter.

Having caught the pony the next thing to do is to fit a halter or headstall and then to tie up to a ring provided for the purpose in a gate post, wall or tree.

The pony should be looked over for injuries. Then lift and pick out the feet at the same time noting the condition of the feet, or, if shod, the shoes. This ensures that the question of reshoeing is not overlooked. Go all over the pony with a dandy brush, brushing off all dry and caked mud. Special attention should be paid to the removal of sweat marks. Then groom the mane and tail with a body brush. End up by sponging out eyes, nostrils and dock. No other attention is necessary.

Certain seasons of the year present problems of their own which call for attention.

Late summer

An abnormally dry summer may result in grassland becoming actually more bare than at any other period of the year. In extreme cases herbage may become so brown or burnt up that no keep for the pony remains. In such cases the pony must be moved where better keep is available, or the feeding of hay instituted as a temporary measure. It must not be forgotten that in a dry summer the normal water supply may also fail.

Mid-winter

Sooner or later in the winter months the time arrives when the feeding of hay, as a supplement to grass, becomes necessary. This ought not to be put off too long or the good condition carried by the pony from the summer will be lost. A thin pony is also a cold pony. In cold weather ponies tend to spend their time sheltering rather than grazing. At such times additional hay keep should be provided or even a small oat or bean feed. Feeding should be done in that part of the field in which the pony elects to shelter. Snow, while causing no acute discomfort to the pony, naturally puts a stop to grazing and the quantity of hay should now be doubled.

The early months of the year, when the coat is at its longest, are also the months of lice infestation. This should be looked for and the necessary action taken to control it (*see page* 243).

Early spring

About the middle of March it is necessary to come to a decision as to what form of grass conservation is to be practised. If the pony is allowed unrestricted access to all the grass land available, then by mid-June little of the growth of grass associated with that time of year will be in evidence. In extreme cases it may be policy to confine the pony to a small paddock and feed hay until the hay crop has been taken.

Early summer

A number of ponies, particularly small ponies, tend to grow too fat during the summer months. This is objectionable in that a fat pony is never a pleasant ride, and it is also dangerous in that an attack of the disease called Laminitis may result (*see page* 233). A pony which shows a tendency to put on too much weight should be moved to a field offering bare keep only so that he gets less to eat and has to move further in search of it.

Flies are a great trial to horses at this time of year. A shelter shed should be made available to them if possible. Failing that, shade and the companionship of another pony so that they stand head to tail and flick away the flies from each other's faces, is appreciated. A docked pony should certainly have access to shelter at this time (*see figure* 44).

FIGURE 44.   A SINGLE AND A DOUBLE SHELTER SHED

Acreages

It is impossible to lay down any hard and fast rules in regard to this as so much depends upon the nature of the soil, quality of the grass, drainage of the land, etc. One acre per pony may be taken as a minimum and two acres per pony as generous, provided the land is in good order. A single pony, however, can scarcely be kept on less than four owing to the necessity to lay up portions of the available grass periodically.

Conservation of land

The keeping of a pony at grass calls for an appreciation of the need for care of land and for its intelligent use. Ponies are among the most wasteful of grazing animals. In their search for the most palatable grasses they trample down and destroy much that is of good feeding value. Furthermore, in the course of time definite portions of the field become so stained with droppings that the grass becomes rank and no longer acceptable as food. It is essential that a long-term plan be adopted if the available land is to be used economically. The following are some of the ways in which waste may be checked or avoided.

The daily removal of droppings by shovel and barrow, is, perhaps, the most effective of all conservation methods. The benefits are undeniable. In default of this, periodical harrowing to spread dung is effective and in this task the pony himself may well be expected to draw a brush harrow and so lend a hand.

The dividing up of land into three parts by fencing, and the grazing of each in turn allows for two portions to be set aside to recover or be renovated whilst a third is in use. This also has the advantage of permitting a part to be laid up from April to June each year for the taking of a hay crop, thereby materially easing the problem of winter keep. The necessity for providing for three sources of water supply and shelter under this plan must not be overlooked.

Fencing

The fencing of land against ponies differs from that for other stock in two essentials. Firstly, the risk of injury is greater and secondly, there is the possibility that the pony will jump the fence. The fencing of choice is post and rails, preferably erected inside existing hedging. The expense of erecting such and the cost of maintenance, however, is high (*see figure* 45A).

Hedges, if tough, strong and well cared for, are the second choice and have the additional advantage of offering wind-breaks and shelter in all weathers. With the exception of yew and deadly nightshade, the hedges of the countryside contain nothing poisonous to horses.

Strands of wire stretched taut between posts also provides an efficient fencing for ponies. The lowest strand should not be less than one foot from the ground or the pony may get his foot over it. The use of barbed wire for this purpose is highly dangerous (*see figures* 45B *&* C).

Electric fencing, which has the advantage of being readily erected where required and dismantled for use elsewhere, is undoubtedly an efficient method.

Hurdles and chestnut paling are not suitable fencing.

The grazing of the land for a period by other types of stock such as bullocks or sheep is also an excellent plan. They eat off grass rejected by ponies and also materially reduce worm parasites in the grass which are dangerous to ponies but harmless to themselves.

Wind-breaks and shelter sheds

Rain may cause ponies to cease grazing, but worries them little otherwise. Snow is a matter of little consequence. It is for shelter from wind that provision ought to be made. Wind-breaks or windscreens formed by thick coppices or even a high hedge on the

FIGURE 45.   A.   POST AND RAILS WITHIN A SHELTER HEDGE

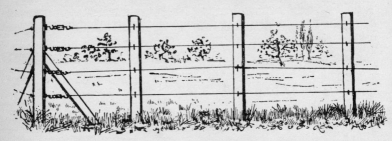

B.   POSTS AND WIRE
The bottom strand must be one foot from ground level

c.   THE KIND OF FENCING NOT SUITABLE FOR HORSES

side of the prevalent wind or north side of the field offer excellent shelter and are generally preferred to a shelter shed.

Shelter sheds, placed in a corner of the field, to which ponies may have access at any time, afford protection against any of the elements. Nevertheless, all experience goes to show that they are seldom resorted to in winter and that real appreciation of them is only shown in summer when they offer protection from the attacks of flies. As such they are fully justified. If built round in shape or with double doorways there is less risk that when two ponies are turned out together one will become "cornered" and injured by the other. It is to be noted that cobwebs ought not to be removed from a shed which is used as a refuge from flies (*see figure* 44).

Rolling

The grass-kept pony has a great advantage over his stabled companion in that he is able to indulge in a roll whenever he feels so inclined.

Why do ponies roll? The reason is by no means clear.

It is undoubtedly done in spring time to help shift the winter coat. It is so frequently done after work that the conclusion is that those parts of the skin subjected to pressure require a rub. It may also be the object to cover wet portions of the coat with dust so as to assist the drying-off process. None of these answers, however, explains why a horse will often roll on a winter's day. It is obvious, however, that rolling is an act of sheer enjoyment, and as such, it must be regarded as both natural and healthy and therefore to be encouraged.

Dogs should be kept to heel when ponies are rolling.

THE COMBINED SYSTEM

By this is understood a system of stable routine which provides for the stabled horse or pony to spend a portion of each day at grass. It is a compromise between the extremes of stabling and grass-keep and in as much as it allows for the best in both systems it has everything to recommend it.

Such a plan is well suited to an animal required frequently for showing, hunting or other purposes, where labour is short and time for regular daily exercise not forthcoming. The rule in such cases is to run him at grass by day and stable at night, excepting only during the heat of summer when the procedure is reversed. Such an arrangement, besides ensuring that the pony is in the stable when required, provides for proper facilities for grooming and corn feeding.

It is under such conditions that the New Zealand rug comes into its own, since it provides the necessary solution to the problem of turning out a clipped animal in winter time.

THE ACCOMMODATION OF PONIES IN CAMP

This is fully dealt with in the Pony Club publication "Camping for the Pony Club".

GROOMING*

Grooming is the daily attention necessary to the coat and the feet of the stabled horse and pony.

The skin is a vital organ, as vital to the horse's health as either his lungs or heart. If a horse is denied the opportunity to live a natural life, to roll and to exercise at will, the skin and feet suffer in consequence unless due care is exercised.

---

*NOTE: This section is also available as a film for teaching purposes, viz. The Pony Club Instructional Film "Grooming".

Objects

> To promote health.
> To maintain condition.
> To prevent disease.
> To ensure cleanliness.
> To improve appearance.

Grooming kit (*see figure* 46)

> *The hoof pick* for cleaning out the feet.
> *The dandy brush* for removing heavy dirt, caked mud and dust.
> It is of special value for use on the grass-kept pony.
> *The body brush* for the removal of dust and scurf from the coat,
> the mane and the tail.
> *The curry comb,* metal or india rubber, for cleaning the body
> brush.
> *The water brush* for use, damp, on the mane, tail and feet.
> *The stable sponge* for cleaning eyes, muzzle and dock.
> *The wisp* for promoting circulation, and for massage.
> *The stable rubber* for a final polish after grooming.

How to groom

The following procedure, though by no means an exhaustive
account of the subject, covers all essential features.

(1) First collect the articles of grooming kit. They are best kept
together in a box or wire basket specially provided for the purpose.
A bucket of water will also be required.

(2) Put the headstall on the horse and remove the rugs. If in
the stable put him on the short rack. It is often pleasanter in summer to take outside and tie him up in a shady spot to a ring,
provided for the purpose in a wall or tree.

(3) Begin by picking out the feet with the *hoof pick*. Pick up each foot in turn; remove whatever may be lodged in the foot with the point of the pick, working downwards from the feet towards the toe. Working this way there is no risk of the pick penetrating the soft parts of the frog. Clear the cleft of the frog and look for any signs of Thrush (*see page* 237). Tap the shoe to see that it is secure, and finally, run the tips of the fingers round the clenches to see that none are risen (*see page* 206).

Hoof Pick   Body Brush   Curry Comb

Dandy Brush   Water Brush   Sponge

Stable Rubber   Wisp

FIGURE 46.   GROOMING KIT

It is permissible, when picking out the feet, to lift the off feet from the near-side, a practice to which ponies soon become accustomed.

It is correct, when picking out, to employ a dung skep to receive the dirt, the skep being placed near enough to allow the dirt to fall directly into it. If however, this is not done, it will be necessary to sweep up afterwards.

(4) Now take the *dandy brush* and begin at the poll on the near side. This brush may be held in either hand as may prove most convenient and is used with a to-and-fro motion. The object is to shift all caked dirt, sweat marks, etc. Thus, certain parts of the body come in for special attention, viz. the saddle region, the belly, the points of the hocks, the fetlocks and pasterns. It is convenient to grasp the tail with the free hand when working on the hind limbs. The use of this brush on the tender parts of the body is best avoided. The Rubber Curry Comb which is now on the market can be used most effectively on the horse in lieu of a dandy brush. It should be used in the same way, and it is also effective for cleaning the body brush.

(5) Now take the *body brush*. The object and also the procedure are now quite different. The short, close-set hairs of the body brush are designed to reach right through the coat to the skin beneath and the brush must be used so that this object is served.

Begin with the mane. First, throw the mane across to the wrong side of the neck and thoroughly brush the crest. Replace the mane and then commence work on it by beginning at the wither end. Insert a finger of the free hand into the mane so as to separate off a few locks of hair. The ends of these are brushed first to remove tangles and then the roots for the same purpose. Work slowly up the neck, dealing with a few locks of hair only at a time.

Now pass to the grooming of the body. Begin at the poll region on the near-side. Take the body brush in the left hand and the curry comb in the right. For the most part it is easier to have the body brush in the left hand when working on the near-side. Stand well back, work with a slightly bent arm and supple wrist and lean the weight of the body behind the brush. The brush is used in short circular strokes in the direction of the lay of the coat and never to-and-fro. After every four or five strokes, draw the brush smartly across the teeth of the curry comb to dislodge the dirt. The curry comb in turn is cleaned by tapping out on the floor, preferably behind the pony and not on the wall or manger. When the near-side has been completed pass to the off-side and change hands.

Now do the head. In a stall or box, the head must be turned away from the manger for this task. The headstall should be dropped and the headstrap fastened temporarily around the neck. Dispense with the curry comb when dealing with the head and use the free hand to steady the pony's head. Work quietly here to avoid injury to tender parts, or knocking bony projections. Horses appreciate gentle grooming of the head but resent rough treatment. Then replace the headstall.

Finally, the tail is dealt with. Here again deal with a few locks of hair only at a time. These may be separated out by holding the tail and shaking a few locks free.

The use of the dandy brush on the mane or tail is wrong as it removes and breaks the hairs leaving them thin and unsightly.

(6) Now take *the wisp*. Wisping is a form of massage to develop and harden muscles, to produce a shine on the coat by squeezing out the oil from the glands in the skin, and to stimulate the skin by improving the blood supply. Damp the wisp slightly and use vigorously by bringing it down with a bang in the direction of the lay of the coat. Give special attention to those parts where the muscles are hard and flat, such as the sides of the neck, the quarters and thighs. Avoid, however, all bony prominences and the tender loin region.

To make a wisp, see page 168.

(7) The *sponge* and bucket of water are next required.

Wring out the sponge so that it is left soft, clean and damp. The eyes receive attention first. Sponge away from the corners and around the eyelids. Wring out the sponge again and deal with the muzzle region, including lips and the inside and outside of the nostrils in that order. Wring out again and move behind the pony to attend to the dock. The tail is lifted as high as possible and the whole dock region, including the skin of the under-surface of the tail, is gently sponged and cleaned. Some owners prefer to maintain two sponges of different colours, one of which is reserved for use in the dock region only.

Sponging refreshes a stabled horse and is appreciated, perhaps, more than any other part of the grooming routine.

(8) "Lay" the mane. This is done by dipping the end hairs of the *water brush* in the bucket of water, shaking and then applying flat to the mane. The hairs are brushed from the roots downwards so that they are left slightly damp and in the desired position.

(9) Wash the feet, using a bucket of water and one end of the water brush for the purpose. The thumb of the hand which holds the foot should be pressed well into the hollow of the heel to prevent water becoming lodged there. Washing feet, however, is by no means essential, and in cold weather is better omitted.

(10) When the hoof is dry go all over it with a small brush dipped in a jar of hoof oil so as to give a thin coating of oil to the whole of the hoof and bulbs of the heel as far up as the coronet. This improves appearance and is beneficial for broken or brittle feet.

(11) Go all over with the *stable rubber* to remove the last traces of dust from the coat. For this purpose the rubber is made up into a flat bundle, damped, and the coat wiped in the direction of the lay of the hair.

(12) Replace rugs and put on a tail bandage.

An experienced groom will spend from half to three-quarters of an hour on the task. A novice will probably need longer because of the fatigue occasioned to unaccustomed muscles. Thoroughness, however, brings its own reward, for few things are more pleasing than a well-groomed horse.

Grooming machines now-a-days are becoming popular. Provided they are used intelligently, they are a boon in a large stable. The correct method of use is to machine-groom every second or third day and to wisp on the intervening days.

The grass-kept pony

Some modification is necessary and desirable in regard to the pony kept at grass. The efficient use of the body brush is scarcely possible on an animal that rolls every day nor can it be employed to any effect on a pony with a long winter coat. The thorough removal of grease and dandruff from the coat of a pony running out, in any case, is wrong as they contribute both to body warmth and the "waterproofing" of the hair. The skin, if a pony is living a natural life, is in a thoroughly healthy condition.

Under such conditions grooming should be limited to attention to the feet, a good brush down with the dandy brush or rubber curry comb to remove mud, attention to mane and tail with the body brush so that they may be kept tidy, and sponging out of eyes, muzzle, and dock. For further information, see the Pony Club publication "Keeping A Pony At Grass".

When to Groom

(1) *Quartering*. Done first thing in the morning. The feet are picked out. The eyes, nostrils and dock are sponged. Rugs are then thrown up or unbuckled in front and turned back. The parts of the body so exposed receive a quick brush down. Particular

attention is paid on this occasion to the removal of stains on the flanks occasioned by lying down at night, the sponge or the water brush being used for this purpose. The object is to make the horse look tidy before morning exercise and to give those parts of the coat which have to be damped in the removal of stains, a chance to dry off before the pony goes out. Note that the whole is carried out without undoing or removing the roller or surcingle.

(2) *Strapping*. This comprises the thorough grooming according to the procedure given earlier in this chapter, the whole of which is carried through from beginning to end. It is preferably done on return from exercise. Grooming can always be carried out more efficiently after a horse has been exercised rather than before, since exercise warms up the skin, loosens and raises the scurf to the surface and opens up the pores. If, however, a horse is fed on return from exercise, a short time should be allowed for him to take his feed undisturbed.

(3) *Brush-over or set-fair*. In the evening the horse is given a light brush over and wisping when the rugs are being changed and the box set fair.

Feet should be picked out several times a day. This should certainly be done on first going to the pony in the morning and at any other time too, as may seem necessary. In order to prevent the littering of the stable paths or yard, feet should be picked out when a horse or pony leaves his box or stall.

How to make a wisp

Make a tightly-woven rope about six to eight feet long by twisting up hay or straw. Soft hay is the best and it should be damped slightly first. Now fashion two loops at one end of the rope, one slightly longer than the other. Twist each loop in turn beneath the remainder of the rope until all is used up. The far end of the rope should then be twisted through the end of each loop and finally tucked away beneath the last twist (*see figure* 47).

A properly made wisp should be hard and firm and no larger than can conveniently be grasped by the hand.

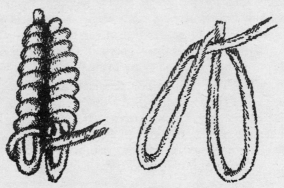

FIGURE 47.   HOW TO MAKE A WISP

CLIPPING AND TRIMMING
CLIPPING

Objects

The reasons for clipping a horse include the following:—

To enable a horse to carry out fast work without undue distress.

To conserve condition by avoiding heavy sweating.

To permit a horse to work longer, faster and better.

To facilitate quicker "drying-off" on return from work.

To save labour in grooming.

To prevent disease.

Equipment

The clipping machines in common use for the purpose are: (1) hand clippers; (2) wheel machine clippers (now rarely seen) and (3) electric clippers. The first-named are slow and laborious, the second necessitate the presence of a whole-time assistant to turn the wheel. Electric clippers, though expensive, are by far the most satisfactory.

Before commencing to clip a horse it is important to ensure that the machine is well oiled and the knife sharp. A horse is easily upset by a noisy machine or a hot and pulling blade. Periodically, therefore, in the course of the clip, the machine should be cleaned and oiled. In the type of machine clipper which has the motor enclosed in the body of the handle care must be taken to keep the ventilation holes clear or overheating will result.

When to clip

Sometime in September it will be noted that, for the first time for many months that the coat appears dull and rough. This indicates the onset of the change of coat, and from now onwards the winter coat begins to grow. Hence the saying "no horse looks well at blackberry time".

Sufficient time should be allowed for the new coat to become well-established before its removal is contemplated. Actually, horses vary greatly as to the time they require their first clip. Again, some horses grow a much thicker coat than others.

The first clip of the season is usually made sometime in October. Following the first clip the coat continues to grow though never as fully as before, so that more than one clip may be necessary. The second or third clip, however, should not be delayed later than the last week of January. Harness ponies may be clipped at any time throughout the winter months.

Types of clip

The full clip. The whole of the coat is removed.

The hunter clip (see figure 48). The same as the above except that the hair is left on the legs as far as the elbows and thighs and a saddle patch is left on the back. It is claimed for this system, with considerable justification, that the coat left on the legs acts as a protection against cold, mud, cracked heels and injury from thorns, and that the saddle patch saves a sore or scalded back under the saddle.

Many hunters are clipped right out the first time and the legs and saddle mark left at the second clipping. On a common horse this has the advantage of making the legs appear less hairy than would otherwise be the case.

Great care must be exercised in carrying out this clip neatly, particularly the saddle patch. If it is too far forward the horse will look short in the shoulder and long in the back. However, if it is cut straight behind the shoulder and allowed to come well back behind the saddle it will often greatly improve the appearance of the animal.

The blanket clip, in which the hair is removed only from the neck and belly, a patch corresponding to that of a blanket, being left on the body.

The trace high clip (*see figure* 49), in which the hair is removed from the belly only, as far up as the traces and from the legs as far as half way down the forearm and thighs. Sometimes the hair immediately beneath the neck is removed also. This clip is useful in the case of ponies kept at grass and is a compromise between clipping partly and not clipping at all. It is a common form of clip for harness ponies.

How to clip

As this, under any system, is a lengthy process, time must be set aside for the task and the necessary assistance arranged. The coat must be dry and as well-groomed as its length will permit. As much of the horse as possible should be clipped without upsetting him or resorting to any means of restraint. The start

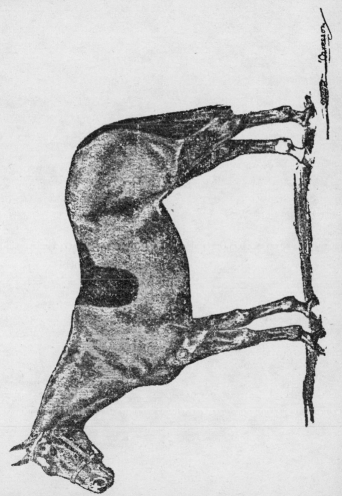

FIGURE 48. A HUNTER CLIP

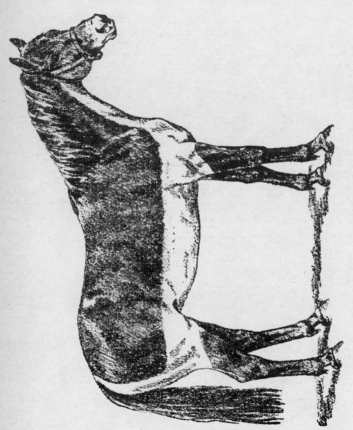

FIGURE 49.   A TRACE HIGH CLIP

may be made anywhere, but in a nervous horse commence at the shoulder region. The most difficult parts to clip both from the point of view of resistance of the animal and favourable results are the head, groin and belly regions.

On no account must hair be removed from the inside of the ears. Long hair in the muzzle region should not be interfered with.

When dealing with the legs use a clipper head with a broader blade called a leg knife. It does not cut off the hair so close.

Care must be taken not to clip the sides of the mane or the root of the tail. The practice of removing a short portion of the mane in the wither region is not recommended.

As clipping proceeds throw a folded rug over the loins. A cold pony soon gets fidgety. Allow the pony to feed from a hay net while clipping everywhere except the head so that he will not fidget or get bored.

The use of clippers is not recommended on the back of the tendons or fetlocks. If they are used the appearance of the legs will be spoilt for some weeks. Skilful use of "trimming" scissors and a comb may be employed when the hair does not pull easily. The comb and scissors must be moved upwards, i.e. against the hair in the same way that a hairdresser trims a head of hair.

TRIMMING

The hairs of the mane and tail will pluck easier when the pores of the skin are warm and open, i.e. after exercise or on a warm day. Many a horse will fidget and it may cause pain if pulling is done in very cold weather when the pores of the skin are tight shut.

The mane

Pulling is done to thin out an over-thick mane, to reduce a long mane to the required length, or to permit the mane to lie flat. The longest hairs from underneath should be dealt with first and removed a few at a time by winding round the finger. The whole operation need not necessarily be completed at one time. Never pull the top hairs, nor any hairs that may stand up after plaiting because they will form an upright fringe on the crest. On no account must scissors or clippers be employed for this purpose.

Hogging the mane is the complete removal of the mane by means of clippers. It is done when a horse or pony grows a ragged mane that spoils the appearance, or when it is desired to eliminate the work involved in the care of a mane. Hogging can only be neatly done with the head lowered and the crest stretched, by getting an assistant to stand in front taking hold of the ears and gently forcing the head down. Clippers are then used to remove the whole of the mane, beginning at the wither end and working upwards towards the poll. Care must be taken that no unsightly line is left where the coat meets the crest. Hogging needs to be repeated about every three weeks.

A mane that has once been hogged will not grow sufficiently to be neat, under two years, and even then may never again regain its former appearance.

Plaiting. Plaiting is done for neatness, to show off the neck and crest and to train the mane to fall to the side desired, normally the off-side of the neck. The number of plaits should be six including the forelock. If more are necessary there should always be an even number including the forelock. There are several ways of putting up a mane. The following are two of the easiest methods.

First method. Required: a water brush, some pieces of thread about eight inches long, a needle with a large eye, a mane comb and a pair of scissors. First damp down the mane with a wet brush and roughly divide into five equal parts. The plaiting of each division should now commence and when three parts of the way down a piece of thread should be taken at its middle and plaited in. When a plait is completed the ends of the thread should be looped round the plait and pulled tight. Having completed all the plaits, ensure that they are all practically of even length. If one is considerably longer than the others make a further loop over. Now take the needle, thread both ends of the thread through the eye, and doubling the end of the plait under, push the needle through the plait from underneath and close to the crest. Pull the ends of the thread through, remove the needle and bind the thread tightly round the

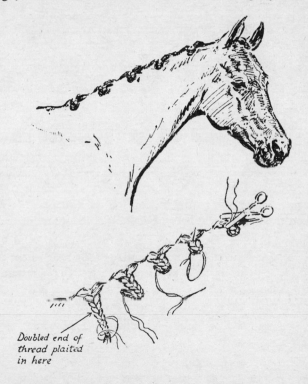

*Doubled end of
thread plaited
in here*

FIGURE 50.   MANE PLAITING

plait. Finish by knotting the thread on the top of the plait and cutting off the spare ends with scissors (*see figure* 50).

Second method. An india-rubber band is used instead of needle and thread. Having finished a long plait, loop the band several times round the end. Then turn the end of the plait underneath into the required position and loop the band around the whole until tight.

The tail

Most horsemen consider that a well-pulled and tidy tail adds greatly to appearance. Tail pulling, however, must be considered undesirable in a pony living at grass as this deprives it of natural protection in the dock region. For tail pulling the following are required: a body brush and a water brush, a mane comb, trimming scissors and a tail bandage.

First groom the tail well to remove all tangles and to separate out the hair. Commence pulling at the dock region by removing all the hair underneath. Then work sideways removing the hair evenly on both sides of the tail. A few hairs only at a time should be removed with the fingers giving a short sharp pull. A little resin on the fingers may help. Further procedure depends upon the type of tail desired.

A bang tail. The end is cut off square at the level of the points of the hocks. Cutting is done with the help of an assistant who places his arm beneath the root of the tail. The cut is then square when the tail is carried naturally (*see figure* 51A).

A long tail collects mud, is difficult to prevent becoming straggly and hides the hocks.

A switch tail. Here pulling is continued drastically to the extent of about half the length of the tail. The ends of the tail are allowed to grow in a natural point (*see figure* 51B).

Horse clippers should never be used on tails. The mane comb breaks and tears the hair and should, therefore, only be employed on a thick and tangled tail, as for example, in a horse just up from grass.

After pulling, the tail should be bandaged in the manner described on page 148. The regular use of stockinette bandages on the dock region greatly assists the preservation of the effect desired.

FIGURE 51A
A Bang Tail

FIGURE 51B
A Switch Tail

Tail plaiting

This is a useful alternative to tail pulling in horses that resent that procedure, for those with an untidy "bushy" tail and for horses kept at grass. Plaiting the long hairs of the dock region makes for neatness and tidiness without depriving the pony of the protection the full tail affords.

The procedure is as follows: the tail hairs at the dock are allowed to grow long. A small number are separated with the finger and thumb on either side of the tail and knotted together with thread. This knot hangs down the cente of the tail and succeeding bunches from either side are plaited in with it. Plaiting in this manner continues downwards for about two thirds of the length of the dock. Thereafter plaiting is confined to the centre hairs of the tail only with which the above knot is incorporated so that a free hanging "pigtail" is formed. When the end of the

FIGURE 52.   TAIL BANDAGING AND TAIL PLAITING

pigtail is reached it is secured with thread and looped back under itself as far as the point where the side hairs ceased to be included. The resulting loop, is stitched together to form a double thickness plait.

Tail washing

Required: A bucket of warm water; a cake of hard yellow soap (soft soap must on no account be used); and two body brushes, one clean. The procedure is as follows: First groom the tail well to remove all tangles. Wet and shampoo using the cake of yellow soap and plenty of finger work. Change the water and rinse well. In a quiet pony the end of the tail may with advantage be immersed in the bucket. Squeeze out the water with the hands and then swing the tail to dislodge any water remaining. Do not bend the hairs. Finally, brush out the tail using a clean body brush, a few hairs at a time and vertically. This will clear the scurf remaining. Finally bandage with a dry tail bandage.

The coat

Some weeks after a horse has been clipped it will be found that long hairs, known as "cat hairs", appear in various parts of the coat, giving an untidy appearance to the pony.

"Singeing"used to be the method employed for their removal, this being done by the flame of a special lamp called a "singeing lamp". The task is better left to the expert. Today electric clippers answer equally well.

Long hairs which grow in the jowl regions and at the back of the tendons may be removed by plucking with the fingers, a few being removed at each grooming.

FEEDING

"The eye of the master maketh the horse fat"

Our ability to feed the stabled horse successfully on a dry and highly concentrated diet is a specialised art, which has been developed and perfected over many generations, as the result of practical experience and scientific study. The good horseman should not be content merely to know what is the right way in which to feed, but should have some understanding of the reasons why.

Grazing is the natural system of feeding and grass the natural food; eating a little at a time and throughout most of the day or night is the natural method. Hence we find that the horse has a remarkably small stomach, the intention being that there should be a little in the stomach all the time and never a lot at any time.

In the successful adjustment of the natural to the artificial, lies the whole art of feeding the stabled horse and pony.

The rules of good feeding

These, which should be known to every horseman, are as follows:—

(1) *Feed little and often* in imitation of the natural method as far as possible. There are, of course, practical limitations to this, but the tables given on pages 192 to 194 show some of the ways in which a compromise may be arrived at.

(2) *Feed plenty of bulk food* (hay) so that, as in grazing, the digestive organs are always well filled. A successful digestive process in the pony is impossible without adequate bulk.

(3) *Feed according to the work done* where concentrated food (oats) is concerned. Increase if the demands of work are heavy; reduce if they become light; stop if the pony has to be laid up but remember to increase the bulk food to compensate for lack of concentrates.

(4) *Make no sudden change in the type of food* or in the routine of feeding. All adjustments must be gradual and spread over several days.

(5) *Keep to the same feeding hours daily.*

(6) *Feed clean and good quality forage only.* The horse is a fastidious feeder and will relish only the best. Musty and dusty fodder not only adversely affect condition but often prove actually harmful.

(7) *Feed something succulent every day* if possible (green food) to compensate for the loss of grass.

(8) *Do not work fast immediately after a full feed or when the stomach is full of grass.* The stomach lies next to the chest and so will press on the lungs when full and so affect the pony's breathing.

(9) *Water before feeding* so that undigested food is not washed out of the stomach. When water is kept continuously in the stable a pony will frequently take a short drink during, or after, a feed. This will do no harm as it does not amount to a long draught.

FORAGE

Concentrated foods

Oats. All experience goes to show that oats are the grain of choice for the horse. They offer a balanced, nutritive and readily digested food on which horses do well. Oats may be fed either whole, bruised or boiled. Provided the oats are fat, plump and clean there is little to choose between the black oat and the white.

Digestion is aided if oats are fed bruised or crushed but owing to the loss of the floury content "crushing" ought not to be carried to the point of the oat being "rolled". An oat crusher forms part of the equipment of all high-class stables.

The feeding of oats to small ponies calls for considerable discretion and as a general rule they are better without them. Small ponies respond rapidly to the highly concentrated feed oats afford and may in consequence become unmanageable or unrideable.

Other grains. In comparison with oats, other grains come rather a poor second. *Barley and flaked maize* are fed with success in parts of the world and in some countries form the staple diet. Boiled barley is sometimes added to the feed to tempt a delicate feeder, to add variety to the diet of a stale or overworked horse and for fattening purposes. *Beans* are extremely nutritious but they are very heating. They should only be given to ponies in small quantities, a double handful given twice a day and mixed with the ordinary feed is usually sufficient. Before feeding they should be "bruised" or split with a hammer. Beans are a useful feed to ponies working off grass in winter time. *Wheat* is a thoroughly bad food and should be avoided.

Horse and pony cubes. As an article of diet these enjoy an increasing popularity amongst horse owners today. They are a compound of a variety of ingredients including oats, bran, maize, barley, locust bean, linseed cake, groundnut meal, grass meal, molasses, etc. plus vitamins and minerals. The composition varies according to the make and the fluctuations of the grain market.

Cubes may be substituted in part or whole for the oat ration, 1 lb. to 1½ lb. of cubes replacing 1 lb. of oats.

The feeding of cubes has many advantages. It saves the storage of several different kinds of grain; it saves the mixing of feeds and ensures that the pony gets a standardised mixed balanced diet with the necessary vitamins and minerals, included. Again ponies fed cubes are far less likely to "hot up" than when fed oats only. The objections are that they are relatively expensive and that their low moisture content may lead to choking unless adequate water is made available. An additive such as chaff or bran fed with them ensures adequate mastication and salivation to moisten them before swallowing.

Bulk foods

Hay offers all that can possibly be required as a bulk food and substitute for grass. That it should prove so eminently satisfactory is perhaps, understandable. Four kinds of hay are commonly fed to horses, namely: *Sainfoin* or *Timothy, Clover, Mixture* and *Meadow*. Of these, Sainfoin is probably the best and is highly nutritious. The stalks are somewhat coarse but this does not appear to be a drawback. Clover hay, though rich, is often very dusty and is susceptible to mould. It is also rather wasteful as much is lost in transit or falls through the hay net. Mixture hay, comprising rye grass, clovers and trefoil, is taken from reseeded land and provides an excellent feed for horses. Meadow hay, on the other hand, comes from pastures permanently laid down to grass and may differ considerably in value. That taken from upland meadows is the best in contrast to that from lowland or water meadows liable to flood.

A good sample of meadow hay should be hard and crisp to feel and sweet to smell (termed its "nose"). The colour should be greenish to brownish. A *yellow* or dark brown colour denotes deterioration, the latter being sometimes due to over heating in the rick, i.e. "mowburnt". Clover or sainfoin hay well-harvested should be golden. Soft hay is always of inferior feeding value. Musty and mouldy hay is harmful and quite unfit for feeding to horses. *New hay,* i.e. that less than six months old, is better avoided as it sometimes proves indigestible. *Old seed* hay should preferably be in the stack twelve months and meadow hay preferably eighteen months. Good old hay provides excellent keep for small stabled ponies.

Other bulk foods. Oat straw is sometimes employed as a substitute for hay or a portion of the bulk feed. It is more suitable for heavy horses though a limited quantity is often added to the hay when making chaff (*see page* 191). The straw of spring sown oats is palatable and readily taken by ponies, being thinner than straw which has been growing all through the winter. Its nutritive value, however, is small and indeed its feeding value lies almost entirely in the bulk it provides, thereby leading to better digestion of the oat ration. Wheat and barley straw are not suitable food for horses.

Other feeding stuffs

Bran is a valuable article of forage for ponies. It may be fed either as an addition to the oat ration, to which it gives bulk, or alternatively damp, as a bran mash. A bran mash has laxative properties and is thus of special value for a sick pony or one suddenly thrown out of work. The practice of feeding a bran mash once a week to stabled horses has everything to recommend it.

To make a bran mash fill a stable bucket about two-thirds full of bran. Pour boiling water over the bran and stir until thoroughly wet. Then cover with a sack and feed when cool enough to eat. If correctly made, the mash should be "crumble-dry", not stiff, and not thin and watery. The mash is more appetising if a little salt or some boiled linseed or two tablespoonsful of treacle or molasses or a handful of oats is added.

Linseed is fed to ponies generally during the winter months only, to improve condition and to give a gloss to the coat. Both effects result from its high oil content. Linseed can be prepared and fed either as "jelly" or "tea". The daily allowance is $\frac{1}{2}$ to 1 lb. of the seed before cooking. Horses cannot absorb more.

Linseed jelly. A special saucepan should be set aside for this purpose. Each evening place a handful of linseed in the saucepan, cover with water and allow to soak with the lid on until the next day. This is best done in the cool oven of the kitchen range. The next evening add more water and bring to the boil. This is important, as soaked, unboiled linseed sometimes proves poisonous. Set aside and allow to cool. If properly made the linseed should set as a jelly, which is then tipped out and mixed with the evening feed. Linseed used in this way needs to be fed daily for at least a fortnight for its benefits to be apparent.

Linseed tea. The preparation of linseed tea is the same as the foregoing except that more water is used. The water in which the linseed is cooked is highly nutritious, and is employed with bran to make a linseed mash.

Linseed cake, though more correctly a cattle food, is much relished by ponies, and if available, may with advantage, be added to the evening feed. If used, it should be fed dry and crushed or in the form of nuts.

Gruel is often offered to ponies on return from a hard day's work as a "pick-me-up" to a tired body (*see page* 217). To prepare gruel place a double handful of oatmeal in a bucket, pour on boiling water, and stir well. Offer when cool. Gruel so prepared must be thin enough for the pony to drink.

Silage up to about one third of the hay ration is occasionally fed to horses.

Grass meal, if of good quality, may be added to the feed of horses not in receipt of grass or other succulents.

Dried sugar beet pulp is popular in some stables but needs to be fed with care since choking may easily result if fed dry. Beet pulp should always be soaked for a period to prevent this and to ensure that it does not swell within the stomach and cause discomfort. Molasses are sometimes added since beet pulp is not very palatable to horses.

Molasses, a by-product in the manufacture of sugar, is used for its nutritional value and also to make other foods more palatable and thus more readily acceptable to a horse. It must never be used to induce a horse to accept inferior quality feeding materials. It is thinned down with warm water and then sprinkled or sprayed onto the feed or hay or added to a bran mash. It is useful for "dainty" feeders.

Succulent foods

The good feeder should be constantly on the look-out for something succulent, i.e. green or juicy, to add to the pony's feed. Such makes the feed more appetising, gives bulk, provides variety, and in part satisfies the natural craving for grass. Scientifically also, there are strong arguments for doing this, related to the valuable vitamin contents such articles possess.

Green food, such as grass, lucerne, etc. should be readily obtainable in summer, and every effort should be made to provide an allowance. These may be fed either in a hay net or chaffed up with the hay and added to the feed.

Carrots are a particularly acceptable article of diet during the winter months as well as being highly nutritious. Some ponies relish swedes, mangels, turnips, beetroots, or parsnips also. To feed these roots first scrub well under a running tap, which for this purpose may be the warm water tap. Then slice from top to bottom into long "fingers" and mix with the feed. Square or round pieces of root must not be fed as they are liable to become lodged in the throat and so choke the pony. Begin by feeding 1 lb. a day and increase to 2 lb. or even more when the pony is accustomed to them.

Salt in small quantities is a necessary addition to a horse's feed. It may be provided either in the form of a "salt lick" in a special container fixed to the wall of the stable; as a lump of "rock salt" kept in the manger, or a teaspoonful of table salt added to the feed once daily. Either of the first two methods are preferable, the pony being able to lick when he feels he requires salt.

How to feed

The whole of the feeding arrangements must be so planned that they comply with the nine rules of good feeding which have already been given. (*See pages* 180-181.)

It is necessary in the first place to decide how much food the pony requires. This depends upon a variety of circumstances, particularly the conditions under which he is kept, namely: whether stabled or at grass; the amount of work he is doing (Rule 3); and the items that are available for use (Rule 7). Provision must, in any case, be made for the pony to receive an adequate amount of bulk fodder daily (Rule 2).

Having decided this point, the next step is to work out a daily programme that will fit in with the work the pony has to do (Rule 1) and the owner's other duties. This programme must be so arranged that the pony is fed several times in the course of the day and at the same times each day (Rule 5), or has access to grazing so that he feeds himself (Rule 2).

The programme should also give due consideration to the following two points: it takes a pony twenty minutes to eat a full corn feed, and one and a half hours in which to digest it. If the pony is to be fed before work, then he must be fed one and a half hours before he goes out, or alternatively only a small feed offered. Secondly, it takes a pony two hours in which to eat 8 lb. of hay. The bulk of the hay ration is thus best given on return from work, i.e. if a pony works in the morning then the hay feed should be given at mid-day when he is at leisure to eat it quietly. For the same reason the largest portion of the hay ration is always given at night when the horse has several hours in which to consume and digest it.

Specimen feed programmes are given on pages 192 to 194.

Feeding corn. Make up the feed, mix it and take it to the pony. A special container is necessary, a "corn sieve", a shallow open circular tray with a basket-work base, is properly used for this purpose, but a plastic basin or a galvanised iron pail answers almost equally well. The required quantity of oats is placed in the receptacle using a scoop or measure of known capacity. Pony cubes and bran are then added if desired, followed by four large handfuls of chaff with carrots or other additions as may be available. The whole is then damped very slightly with water, mixed well, carried to the pony and tipped into the manger. The pony must then be left undisturbed.

The procedure is the same for ponies at grass in receipt of a corn allowance. The feed is tipped into a feed tin or feed box placed on the ground in some convenient spot (*see figures* 53A *and* 53B). Much jealousy is exhibited when ponies are taking their corn feed and it is important, therefore, that there shall be one feed tin for every pony in the field; that all shall be fed at the same time and that the feed tins be spaced well apart.

FIGURE 53A.   A FEED TIN OF GALVANISED IRON

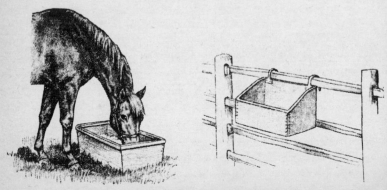

FIGURE 53B.   FEED BOXES

Mangers, feed tins or feed boxes require periodical scrubbing out and airing.

Wasteful feeders, that is to say ponies which throw their feed out of the manger, may be defeated in one of the following ways: a brick or large round stone or, best of all, a large lump of rock salt kept in the manger; bars fitted across the manger at both ends; feed from a nosebag.

Feeding hay. Hay may be fed from specially provided hay racks, either at manger level or eye level. The former are preferable and the latter objectionable in that they necessitate the horse feeding at an unnatural height and that hay seed and dust tend to fall into the eyes or the hollow above the eyes. Today, however, the favoured method of hay feeding is to utilise *hay nets* for the purpose, the popularity of which is due solely to their merits.

The following are among their many advantages: Waste is avoided. Soiling is prevented as the hay is not trampled under foot. Digestion is aided as the horse can only secure a limited amount at a time. Dust and seeds fall through to the ground. They act as a measure. They are cheap, long-lasting, easily filled and easily transported. They are eminently suited to those grooms, who dislike the common practice of carrying hay on a pitchfork over-head. They are equally suited to indoor or outdoor use or during road or rail transportation.

Hay nets should be secured clear of the ground so that when empty the ends are not trodden on. A form of easily released knot should be employed (*figure* 54).

For stable use the hay net is best secured to the short-rack ring. In the open they may be tied to the supporting poles of the fence, a different place being chosen each day to avoid "poaching" of the ground. Here again one net must be provided for each pony in the field and these hung well apart from one another.

Hay nets vary greatly in size and hence in the amount of hay which they contain, which again is affected by the quality of the hay used and the extent to which it is shaken up first. It is a wise plan to fill and weigh nets from time to time to obviate any risk of short feeding.

FIGURE 54.   SHOWING TWO WAYS OF TIEING UP A HAY NET CORRECTLY

Chaff or chop. The hay alone or together with a small proportion of oat straw and any green food available is passed through a "chaff cutter" and then fed with the corn feed. Such adds bulk to the oat feed, ensures slower feeding and better mastication and prevents bolting the food. Chaff cutters form part of the equipment of all high-class stables.

Chaff feeding has, however, somewhat gone out of fashion, partly because few small stables possess a chaff cutter and partly because of the heavy work involved in working the machine. The purchase of chaff ready cut from a corn merchant is unsatisfactory since little control can be exercised as to the quality of the hay used. Bulk can be afforded in other ways such as the inclusion of bran instead.

SPECIMEN FEED TABLES

Type & height	Hunter 16-2 hh.	Hunter 15-2 hh.	Hunter 14-2 hh.	Hunter 14-2 hh.–16-2 hh.
Season ..	Winter	Winter	Winter	Summer
How kept ..	Stabled, clipped and rugged.	Stabled, clipped and rugged.	Part clipped and out by day.	Summering at grass.
Work ..	Hunting 2 days per week.	Hunting 3 days per fortnight.	Hunting 2 days a week.	Nil.
Feed ..	7 a.m. Oats 2 lb., bran 1 lb. with chaff, hay 2 lb. 12 noon. Oats 3 lb., bran 1 lb. with chaff, carrots. 12.30 p.m. Hay 5 lb. 4.30 p.m. Oats 3 lb., bran 1 lb., linseed jelly 1 lb., chaff. 7.30 p.m. Oats 4 lb., bran 1 lb., chaff, hay 7 lb.	7 a.m. Oats 1 lb., cubes 1 lb., bran 1 lb., hay 2 lb. 12 noon. Oats 2 lb., cubes 1 lb., bran 1 lb., carrots. 12.30 p.m. Hay 4 lb. 4.30 p.m. Oats 2 lb., cubes 1 lb., bran 1 lb., linseed jelly 1 lb., chaff. 7.30 p.m. Oats 3 lb., cubes 2 lb., bran 1 lb., hay 7 lb.	7 a.m. Cubes 2 lb., bran 1 lb., hay 4 lb. 10 a.m. Turn out to grass. 4 p.m. Catch up. Oats 2 lb., bran 1 lb., chaff. 7 p.m. Oats 3 lb., cubes 1 lb., bran 1 lb., hay 6 lb.	Grazing only. Late summer:— Oats 2 or 4 lb. or cubes 4 lb. with bran.

SPECIMEN FEED TABLES

Type & height	Show Hack or Jumper 15 hh.	Cob 14-3 hh.	Riding School Hack 14-2 hh.	Child's Pony 13-2 hh.
Season	Summer	Winter	Summer	Winter
How kept	Stabled, clipped and rugged.	Stabled, clipped and rugged.	Stabled by day. Out at night.	Stabled, clipped and rugged.
Work	Show ring and schooling.	Hunting 2 days a week.	School rides, twice daily, six days a week.	Hunting. Pony Club rallies.
Feed	**7 a.m.** Oats 2 lb., bran 1 lb., chaff, hay 2 lb. **12 noon.** Oats 3 lb., bran 1 lb., chaff. **12.30 p.m.** Hay 5 lb. **4.30 p.m.** Oats 4 lb., bran 1 lb., chaff. **7.30 p.m.** Oats 4 lb., bran 1 lb., hay 7 lb. and green food.	**7 a.m.** Oats 1 lb., cubes 2 lb., bran 1 lb., hay 2 lb. **12 noon.** Oats 1 lb., cubes 2 lb., faked maize 1 lb., bran 1 lb. **12.30 p.m.** Hay 4 lb. **5 p.m.** Oats 3 lb., cubes 1 lb., faked maize 1 lb., bran 1 lb., carrots, hay 6 lb.	**6.30 a.m.** Oats 2 lb., cubes 1 lb., flaked maize 1 lb., bran 1 lb., hay 3 lb. **12.30 p.m.** Cubes 2 lb., flaked maize 1 lb., bran 1 lb., hay 4 lb. **4.30 p.m.** Oats 1 lb., cubes 1 lb., flaked maize 1 lb., bran 1 lb. **5 p.m.** Turn out.	**8 a.m.** Cubes 1 lb., bran 1 lb., hay 2 lb. **12.30 p.m.** Cubes 2 lb., bran 1 lb., hay 2 lb. **4 p.m.** Oats 1 lb., cubes 2 lb., bran 1 lb., carrots. **5 p.m.** Hay 5 lb.

SPECIMEN FEED TABLES

Type & height	Child's Pony 13-2 hh.	Child's Pony 12-2 hh.	Child's Pony 13-2 hh.–12-2 hh.	Shetland 38 in.
Season	Summer	Winter	Winter	Winter
How kept	At grass.	By night stabled. By day at grass.	At grass.	At grass.
Work	Pony Club rallies, Shows, Gymkhanas.	Pony Club rallies, Hacking, Hunting.	None (Owner at school).	1 hour a day mounted work.
Feed	8 a.m. Catch up. Cubes 1 lb., bran ½ lb. 4 p.m. (if worked). Cubes 3 lb., bran 1 lb.	8 a.m. Cubes ½ lb., bran ½ lb., hay 3 lb. 10 a.m. Turn out to grass. 4 p.m. Catch up. Cubes ½ lb., bran 1 lb., carrots, hay 5 lb.	10 a.m. Hay 4 lb. 4 p.m. Cubes 2 lb., bran 1 lb., hay 5 lb., carrots.	Winter only: once daily. Cubes ½ lb., bran 1 lb., carrots, hay 6 lb.

The term chaff indicating "chopped hay" must not be confused with the same name applied to the oat glumes resulting in the winnowing of corn.

Feeding in camp

The feeding of ponies in camp is fully dealt with in the Pony Club publication "Camping for The Pony Club".

Storage of forage

If forage is stored in the stable it readily becomes contaminated and soiled. A special forage store ought to be set aside for the purpose. Oats in particular require safeguarding for many a good horse has been lost through getting loose at night and gaining access to the oat supply. Oats should be stored in special bins that afford protection against vermin and which are provided with a lid sufficiently heavy to prevent a horse raising it.

WATERING

The importance of a clean and adequate water supply for the pony cannot be over-stressed. Nothing so quickly adversely affects condition as faulty watering arrangements.

Although under certain conditions ponies will drink stagnant, smelly and discoloured water, they undoubtedly much prefer an absolutely clean and fresh supply from a clean container.

Watering systems

Water trough in the stable yard. This system is useful in the case of horses returning from work to drink from it before going into their stable. It is unsatisfactory in that on other occasions it necessitates taking the horse out of the stable several times a day, a common cause of neglect. In winter time the horse leaves a warm stable for a cold yard.

Water troughs need regular emptying and cleaning

Water bowl in manger. Satisfactory when the bowl is clean and full. Frequently, however, such bowls are allowed to become dirty and empty.

Automatic drinking bowls. These are filled by a lever which the horse operates himself or by gravity. Not all horses will use the former and a common fault to both is shallowness which prevents a deep full drink. They are excellent for stall stables. Special plumbing, however, is necessary, and unless watched they are liable to become clogged. They need to be tested daily.

Bucket in the corner of the box. Probably the most satisfactory system of all. The bucket may either be placed on the floor or suspended in a special ring fitting. Wooden buckets (oak pails) are far the most suitable for this purpose. They last many years, are easy to keep sweet and clean, offer no risk of injury to the horse and are not readily knocked over. Unfortunately, an oak bucket may be too heavy for some grooms to carry when full of water, an objection which may be overcome by providing a stable hosepipe or plastic bucket for filling purposes. Galvanised iron pails, though not so heavy, are less satisfactory. They are readily knocked over when empty and soon go out of shape. India rubber, plastic or heavy polythene buckets are often seen today and have the merits of being long lasting, noiseless and without risk of injury to the pony.

The place of choice for the bucket should be in a corner of the box, away from the manger where the contents may become soiled, away from the door where it may become knocked over but within sight of the door so that it can be viewed easily for cleanliness or emptiness.

Buckets used for watering purposes should be emptied daily, and given a periodical scrubbing and airing to sweeten them. Shortage of water under this system can be insured against by providing two buckets for each box.

Rivers and streams. When ponies are kept at grass it is a great advantage if the field has a stream passing through it. The ideal conditions are running water with a gravel bottom and good approach. A shallow stream with a sandy bottom may result in the pony taking in a small quantity of sand each time he drinks, leading eventually to an accumulation of sand inside him and an attack of sand colic. Streams with a steep bank or a deep muddy approach are unsuitable watering places.

Ponds. If the only water supply available in a field is a pond of stagnant water, then alternative arrangements should be made.

Field troughs. Field troughs filled from a piped supply of water provide the best watering arrangements for the pony at grass. Galvanised iron troughs answer well for this purpose. They should be from 3 ft. to 6 ft. long, about 15 in. deep and placed so that the top is about 2 ft. from the ground. They must be provided with an outlet at the base for emptying. Such troughs should be placed clear of trees so that leaves do not accumulate in them. The ground chosen should be well drained otherwise the surround will become muddy in winter. The nearer the trough is to the house, the gate or the road, the better the chance that it will be regularly inspected. During frost and snow they require attention at least twice daily.

Such troughs are best filled by means of a ball-cock apparatus enclosed in a covered compartment at one end of the trough. The trough then automatically fills whenever the pony drinks. If a tap is made use of, it should be placed at ground level and the piping from there onwards so fitted that it hugs the side and edge of the trough thus offering no projection on which the pony may become caught up. An outlet hole in the side of the trough must be provided so that the level of water is always below that of the inlet pipe. A projecting tap in the vicinity of a trough is highly objectionable.

(a)   A self-filling trough with the ball-cock apparatus in an enclosed compartment.

(b)   Another good arrangement. The tap is so placed that the pony cannot interfere with it and there is no projecting inlet pipe on which he may become caught up. An outlet hole in the side of the trough is necessary to prevent the level of water reaching the end of the inlet pipe.

(c)   A bad arrangement. The sharp edge of the bath will lead to injury to the knee and the projecting tap is dangerous.

FIGURE 55.   FIELD TROUGHS

Field water troughs require regular inspection, emptying and cleaning. On such occasions it is an advantage to leave them empty for a few hours to allow the sun to sweeten them.

When to water

The ideal arrangement provides that the pony shall always have water available to him. In default of this a pony needs watering four times a day in winter, five or six times a day in summer. Water should always be offered first thing in the morning, the bucket being emptied and refilled for the purpose, also on return from work and before feeding. If a pony is permitted a full drink while at work, then he should not be put to a fast pace for at least half an hour afterwards.

No harm results from a pony taking a drink from an ice-covered trough.

Obvious harm seldom shows when a hot and sweating horse takes a full drink of cold water but the circumstances under which a pony should be watered should seldom arise. A pony watered under such conditions should be walked about afterwards.

In the course of a long day's hunting, ponies may, with advantage, be permitted a short drink at a convenient watering place, but a full draught ought not to be allowed if fast work is to follow immediately afterwards.

If ponies know that water is always available in stable and field they will drink as and when necessary and take no harm.

Watering in camp

This is fully dealt with in the Pony Club publication "Camping for the Pony Club"

THE FOOT AND SHOEING*

"No foot—no horse"

Every horseman should have some understanding of the care of a pony's feet and of shoeing. "No foot—no horse" is an old and a very wise saying.

For a proper appreciation of shoeing however, some simple understanding of the structure and function of the various parts of the foot is essential.

STRUCTURE

The foot consists of three parts: the wall, the sole and the frog (*see figure* 56). All three are horny structures and are non-sensitive with neither nerve nor blood supply which explains why shoeing nails can be driven through the wall and why the frog and sole can be cut with a knife without causing pain or bleeding.

The wall. This is the part seen when the foot is on the ground. The wall grows downwards from the coronet, just like a finger-nail, and in the natural state the rate of growth equals the rate of wear of the unshod foot at ground level. The wall goes right round the foot and at the heels is reflected inwards to form the "bars".

The outer surface of the wall is provided with a glistening coat, the object of which is to prevent undue evaporation from the horn so that it will not degenerate and become hard and brittle.

It is customary to speak of the "toe" of the foot, the "quarters" and the "heels".

The sole (*figure* 56) protects the foot from injury from below. Being none too thick for this purpose, liberties cannot be taken

---

*NOTE : This section has been reproduced in greater detail as a film strip lecture and booklet for teaching purposes, viz. "The Foot and Shoeing".

with it. In a healthy state it is slightly concave, i.e. like a saucer turned upside down, such an arrangement affording a better foothold.

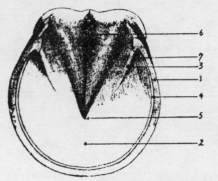

1. The Wall
2. The Sole
3. The Bars
4. The White Line
5. The Point of the Frog
6. The Cleft of the Frog
7. The Seat of Corn

FIGURE 56.   THE PARTS OF THE FOOT

The frog (*figure* 56) is nature's anti-slipping and anti-concussion device. It is the first part of the foot to make contact with the ground thus affording the pony a good foothold and at the same time taking up the jar of impact. The peculiar wedge shape of the frog and its irregular surface with its central "cleft" assist materially in its anti-slipping function. Its power to act as a shock absorber depends upon its size and india-rubber-like consistency, its upward movement and the cushion within the foot on which it rests.

When it is remembered how much lameness is directly attributable to slipping or concussion in the leg, the importance of a healthy frog cannot be overstressed.

The interior of the foot is made up of bones, joints and sensitive structures any or all of which are liable to injury should the wall, sole or frog be penetrated.

SHOEING

The need for shoeing is the direct consequence of domestication, the working of a horse on hard roads leading to wearing away of the wall at a greater rate than it is replaced. Conversely, the effect of shoeing is that the wall is protected from any wear whatsoever and since it still continues to grow the foot becomes unduly long. It will thus be seen that the shod foot calls for care and attention just as much as does the unshod foot.

Systems of shoeing

Two systems are recognised, namely, "hot" shoeing and "cold" shoeing.

In "hot shoeing" the shoe is specially made to fit the foot, it is tried on hot and adjustments are made before it is finally nailed on. A visit to the forge is necessary. In "cold shoeing" a ready-made shoe is employed which is fitted and altered cold as far as is possible. The former, is of course, by far the more satisfactory process.

Hot shoeing

The procedure of reshoeing a pony by this method falls into six definite stages, viz. removal, preparation, forging, fitting, nailing on and finishing.

Removal consists in the removal of the old shoe. The blacksmith first cuts all the clenches by means of his "buffer" and "driving hammer". The shoe is then levered off with his "pincers" (*figure* 57). Provided clenches have been cleanly cut there should be no breaking or tearing away of the wall as the shoe is released.

Preparation comprises reduction of the overgrowth of horn and the adjustment of the foot for the fitting of the new shoe. The smith first cleans out the sole and frog, notes their condition and casts an expert eye over the shape of the foot generally. The overgrowth of wall is removed with his "drawing knife" or "toeing

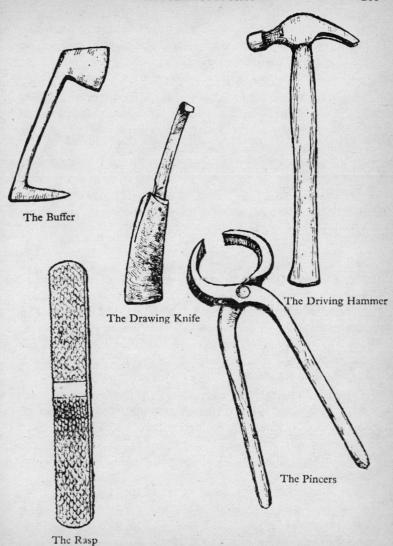

The Buffer

The Drawing Knife

The Driving Hammer

The Pincers

The Rasp

FIGURE 57. A FARRIERS TOOLS

knife", or sometimes with his "horn cutter". Ragged parts of the sole and frog are trimmed away, but for reasons already given undue cutting of sole or frog is avoided. The "rasp" is then taken into use to provide the foot with a level "bearing surface" (*figure* 57).

Forging is the making of the new shoe. The weight and type of iron selected for the purpose depends directly upon the nature of the work required of the pony. After the iron has been shaped the nail holes are "stamped" and clips are "drawn".

Fitting is carried out while the shoe is still hot. The shoe is carried to the foot on a "pritchel". The searing of horn which results reveals exactly the extent to which foot and shoe are in perfect contact. Any adjustments necessary in the shape of the shoe or length of the heels are then made.

Nailing on. The shoe is cooled by immersion in water and nailed on, the first nail to be "driven" being usually one of the toe nails. Nails used for this purpose are of special design and are provided with a special form of head which always fills the nail hole however much the shoe may wear away. Nails are made in various sizes and it is important that the right size nail is used. If too large, the head will project and wear away too soon. If too small, the head will not properly fill the nail hole. The one fault is as bad as the other for both result in early loosening of the shoe.

The end of the nail, where it penetrates the wall, is turned over and twisted off leaving a small piece projecting called the "clench". "Fine nailing" is where the nail penetrates too little of the wall so affording an insecure hold. "Coarse nailing" is where the nail comes out too high up the wall. The risk here is that the nail may be driven too close to sensitive structures, i.e. "nail binding", or actually into sensitive structures—"pricked foot".

Clips, generally one toe clip for a fore shoe and two quarter clips for a hind shoe, assist in keeping the shoe in position and also afford greater security.

Finishing. The clenches are tidied up with the rasp and a small "bed" made for them in the wall beneath, after which they are "embedded". The toe clip is tapped lightly back into position. Finally, the rasp is run around the extremity of the wall where horn and shoe meet to reduce any risk of cracking.

What to look for in a newly-shod foot

(1) That the shoe has been made to fit the foot and not the foot to fit the shoe, i.e. that the wall has not been rasped away to meet the iron and that the toe has not been "dumped". Such abuse, inasmuch as it removes the surface coat of the wall, inevitably leads to cracking and breaking away of the rasped portions.

(2) That the type of shoe provided is suitable to the work required of the pony.

(3) That the weight of iron chosen is in proper relation to the size of the horse or pony.

(4) That the foot has been suitably reduced in length at both toe and heel and evenly so to both inside and outside.

(5) That there has been no abuse of the knife on either sole or frog.

(6) That the frog is in contact with the ground.

(7) That sufficient nails have been used, not too many and not too few. The normal number is three on the inside and four on the outside.

(8) That the right size of nail has been used and that the heads have been driven home and fill the nail holes.

(9) That the clenches are well formed, in line and the right distance up the wall.

(10) That no daylight shows between shoe and foot, particularly at the heel region.

(11) That the heels of the shoe are not too long nor too short.

(12) That the place for the clip has been neatly cut and that the clip has been well-drawn and well-fitted.

Reshoeing

As a general rule a shod pony should be taken to the forge once a month. Even if the shoes are not badly worn there will then be a sufficient growth of horn to call for its reduction. This is particularly true of the toe region and a pony with an overlong toe is always liable to stumble.

"Removes" are the procedure by which a slightly worn shoe is taken off, the foot reduced in length and the same shoe replaced.

A pony subjected to heavy work on hard roads may well wear his shoes through in less than a month and in such cases visits to the forge need to be more frequent.

The indications that a pony is overdue for reshoeing are as follows:—

(1) The shoe is loose.

(2) Any part of the shoe has worn thin.

(3) The clenches have "risen" and stand out from the wall

(4) The foot is overlong and out of shape.

(5) A shoe has been "cast", i.e. lost.

Types of shoes

The plain stamped. This is a horse shoe in its simplest form. It consists of an unmodified bar of iron, shaped, stamped with nail holes and provided with a toe clip. Such shoes are only suitable for horses doing relatively slow work since they possess no provision against "slipping" or "interfering".

The hunter shoe (*figures* 58 *and* 59). This is a drastically modified form of the above, designed to meet the needs of a horse or pony moving at a fast pace on grass and pulling up short. Such shoes are made of "concave" iron to reduce the risk of suction in soft going and to offer a more secure grip on the ground. The ground surface is "fullered", i.e. provided with a groove, to provide a better foothold. In the fore shoe the heels are "pencilled" to avoid the risk of their being caught by the hind shoe and pulled off. On the hind shoe the toe is "rolled", i.e. the toe is set back and bevelled off, to minimise the risk and consequences of "over-reaching" and quarter clips are provided to allow for the rolling of the toe. The outer heel is provided with a "calkin" to afford greater control in pulling up and the inner heel has a "wedge" for similar reasons, a wedge being less likely to cause "brushing" than a calkin.

FIGURE 58.   A HUNTER FORE SHOE   FIGURE 59.   A HUNTER HIND SHOE

Although primarily intended for the shoeing of hunters, this type of shoe is eminently suited to any horse or pony doing fast work on grass, viz. paperchases, showing, jumping and gymkhanas.

Anti-brushing shoes (*figure* 60) are used for ponies that hit and injure the opposite leg, i.e. "brushing". The inner branch of such shoes is "feathered" and fitted close in under the wall so that the risk of striking the opposite leg is reduced to a minimum. There are no nail holes in the inner branch of such shoes.

FIGURE 60.   A FEATHER EDGED SHOE

Grass tips (*figure* 61) are thin half-length shoes used on hunters when running at grass to protect the wall in the toe region from splitting. They permit the frog to come into full action during the run at grass and thus assist materially in maintaining its healthy state.

Heel studs. Studs made of special metal are now obtainable for fitting into the heels of shoes. Such afford a considerable measure of additional security against slipping in that the metal of the stud being slower wearing than that of the shoe always presents a roughened surface to the ground.

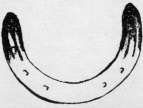

FIGURE 61.   A GRASS TIP

Working unshod

This is quite a feasible proposition provided work on hard gritty roads or flinty tracks is avoided. Not only is there a saving in shoeing charges and visits to the forge, but an unshod pony is more secure on every type of surface and hence more surefooted. Furthermore, the injury resulting from a kick is materially lessened.

The changeover from working shod to working unshod must be a gradual process. Once it is understood that additional wear is expected of wall and sole, nature will respond and throw out a harder and firmer horn to meet the additional demands. This, however, takes time, and until the harder horn has developed care must be taken not to work the pony to the point at which he becomes footsore.

The feet of ponies worked unshod need to receive regular attention from the blacksmith so that a level ground surface to the foot is maintained and splitting and cracking of the wall checked.

HEALTH, CONDITION AND EXERCISE

HEALTH

The "indications of health" in the horse and pony are as follows, and should be known to every horseman.

The head is on the alert, eyes wide open, ears pricking to and fro. The lining of the eyes and nostrils is a salmon-pink colour. The pony feeds up well. The coat is smooth and glossy and easily moved on the ribs beneath. The pony stands evenly on all four feet; a hind foot may be rested alternately but never a fore foot. Droppings are passed about eight times daily and are formed into balls which break on hitting the ground. Urine, which is thick and light yellow in colour, is passed several times a day. The temperature is normal, viz. 100·5 degrees, and respirations are about 10 to 12 to the minute.

CONDITION

A horse or pony is said to be in "soft" condition when his muscles are slack, he is fat, has a gross belly and is incapable of sustained effort without sweating and distress. Unexercised horses at grass in summer are in "soft" condition.

A horse or pony is said to be in "hard" condition when he is free of superfluous fat both inside and out and his muscles and tendons are toned up to withstand sustained effort without injury or distress. A hunter in regular work in winter is in "hard" condition.

Fatness versus fitness

It is necessary to have a clear conception of the difference between these two, and its significance. The fat, round, sleek appearance of a pony at grass, though indicative of perfect health, is no criterion as to the pony's physical fitness to undertake work. In such a pony the muscles are soft and flabby and in an unfit state to withstand physical exertion. This applies to all muscles, those of the heart and lungs just as much as those of the limbs. The belly is large and occupies an undue proportion of the frame so that lung space is restricted. Such is fat condition.

Fitness, on the other hand, is the condition of the pony in hard work, whereby he is able and capable of undertaking physical exertion without detriment to his health. Such physical effort may be in the form of sharp bursts of energy as, for example, in racing, horse trials and polo; prolonged sustained effort as, for example, in hunting and driving; or slow steady exertion over long periods, as, for example, in trekking and expeditions.

The essentials in all cases are the same, namely, that the muscles of the limbs shall stand up to the strain imposed upon them without becoming tired or breaking down; that the muscles of the heart are equal to every demand and that the muscles of the chest permit full and free respiratory powers. In such a pony the gross belly of the fat pony has given place to something more modest that does not press on the chest and interfere with free breathing, thus giving the lungs greater space in which to work.

To "condition" a hunter

To convert a pony from "soft" condition to "hard" condition two essentials are necessary, namely, sufficient work, combined with the correct amount of food. Only so can muscles be toned up to their task, the belly reduced and heart and lungs brought into perfect working order. Hunters are subjected to this process each autumn when brought up soft from grass and prepared for the work of the hunting season. Some form of conditioning is also necessary with a child's pony at grass during the owner's absence at school if the pony is to be ready and fit to undertake the tasks to be asked of it in the school holidays.

The procedure for conditioning a horse or pony is as follows: Shoe up first of all, then put into walking work daily for a week. Watch carefully for signs of galling under the saddle or girth. Next combine walking with slow trotting. Increase the grain feed in proportion to the work. If properly carried out there will be an increase in muscle at the expense of belly. The profuse lathery sweat of the soft animal gives place to a slight dampness or none at all. The whole must be a gradual undertaking and in the case of a hunter can hardly be accomplished in less than six weeks.

EXERCISE

The laborious process of getting a pony into hard condition is wasted if the pony is thrown out of work. For maintenance of condition, exercise is essential. Such calls for the exhibition of a considerable measure of common sense. A pony that has hunted hard on Monday does not require two hours exercise on Tuesday. A quiet walk round for twenty minutes to take stiffness out of joints or swelling out of legs is all that is necessary. If, however, the pony is not to hunt again until the following Monday then exercise or work during the intervening period is essential if hard condition is to be maintained. Such may amount to about two hours daily whether led or ridden, but on some days the pony ought certainly to be saddled and ridden so that the back and girth regions may also be kept hard.

A perfect exercising track is difficult to find but the ideal will include a long gradual incline over grass. A long steady uphill trot on such provides everything necessary to muscle up quarters and keep wind right. Some road work is advisable also.

The amount of exercise given need not necessarily be the same every day nor need the pace be fixed. The value of slow steady exercise, i.e. hound-jogging, is emphasised. Neither galloping nor fast trotting will get or keep a pony fit, indeed they may only do harm. Finally, the route chosen should be varied, which in this instance is an exception to the rule given elsewhere to adhere to a fixed daily routine whenever possible.

Exercise versus work

It is necessary here to differentiate between work and exercise, as understood in a well-conducted hunting stable. The word "exercise" denotes the process of giving a horse or pony sufficient exercise in order to keep him healthy and fit without causing him any undue exertion, or causing him to lose any condition. The general procedure would be prolonged periods at a steady jog on sound and safe going, conducted by a groom.

The word "work" would denote the owner riding for his pleasure, and would include, besides hunting, etc., canters, gallops, school work, jumping, all of which might be expected to cause the pony some effort. Exercise and work must be co-ordinated to produce a fit trained pony.

The provision of exercise under conditions in which frost and snow put a stop to hunting presents a problem, since neither country nor roads are rideable. A solution may be found in laying down a circular straw track for the purpose.

In winter time the need for adequate exercise for the stabled pony is of greater importance than for the pony kept at grass, for in the latter case, to a very great extent, liberty in a field, when keep is poor, with consequent continuous use of limbs combined with an occasional gallop round, in themselves keep the pony partly muscled up, and his wind right. This accounts for the fact that the hunter kept at grass during term time, may be reasonably hard when wanted in the holidays if it has been given good hay and a corn feed once a day.

Roughing-off

By this is understood the process whereby a fit pony on being taken out of work at the end of the season, is prepared for a rest at grass (i.e. "the summering of hunters"). The points for attention are as follows: Stop all exercise, grooming and corn feeding; mash down for a few days; get the blacksmith to remove the shoes and trim the feet.

Choose a mild day to turn out and always turn out early in the day so that the pony can inspect his field and its fences and find his watering point in daylight.

THE CARE OF THE HUNTER ON A HUNTING DAY

and

THE CARE OF A PONY ON THE DAY OF A PONY CLUB RALLY

THE CORN-FED, CLIPPED-OUT AND STABLED PONY

Early morning. Be up in good time and go to the stables at least an hour before breakfast. Then look round the pony as usual, water and tie up a small net of hay. Pick out feet, muck-out, rearrange bedding and "set fair" as there will be no time to do so later. Quarter or groom as time permits, plait the mane, put a tail bandage on, feed and leave the pony on the short-rack. Check up saddlery, which should have been put ready the previous day. Then go to breakfast.

The start. Judge the time of departure by aiming to journey at six miles an hour.

After breakfast return to the stable, prepare the evening feed, hay net and gruel if possible, see that the pony has cleared up his feed though some ponies, when excited by anticipation may not always "clear up". In this matter you will soon get to learn your pony's habits. Remove clothing, saddle up, mount, test the saddle against any pressure on the spine, and move off at a walk for five minutes, until all is settled. Then adjust girths. The object now is to cause your mount as little fatigue as possible on the way to your destination, and it is now that you will benefit if you are riding a well-trained and well-mannered pony. A good walk and level cadenced trot are easy paces for mount and man, and both paces can be used as condition of road surface and gradient dictate. A well-schooled pony will expend little energy in a quiet canter on grass, but it does not look well to arrive at a Meet or Rally with your well-turned-out pony sweating and muddy.

On arrival. Dismount, look round your pony, check shoes and make any necessary adjustments to your saddlery. Keep well clear of other horses' heels. If the weather is cold, remount and walk about in order to keep your pony warm.

Riding to hounds is a subject upon which much has been written. Suffice it to say that the time has now come to reap the reward of all that has been done for weeks past to turn the pony out a credit to yourself, to the Hunt which you support and to the Branch of the Pony Club to which you belong.

If the work has been well done then the pony will be in hard galloping condition and equal to any demand required of him. The fact that the pony is hard and fit and keen is not, however, to be made an excuse for galloping about without cause and jumping unnecessarily, nor in any other way expending his energy foolishly.

Take advantage of good going when it offers itself; turn the horse's head to the wind if he is blowing hard at a check; as opportunity permits be very quick to dismount and have a look round, thus easing the weight off the back for a moment; be quiet with the hands and aids; sit well with the pony at all paces.

At a rally do as above until an instructor tells you otherwise. Once under instruction, or when moved off from the Meet, the task in hand becomes the first consideration while the care of the pony, though still important, takes second place.

The road home. The hunt or rally finished, the care of the pony again becomes the matter of first consideration.

The object for pony and rider must be to get home in a cool state, as quickly as possible, without causing any further undue fatigue.

Firstly, then aim at cooling off, mentally and physically. Take the quickest and easiest route. Loosen girths slightly and ride on a long rein, but do not dawdle. When the pony is cooled down allow him to rinse his mouth out at a stream, pond or cattle trough if met with. Your pace and route must be governed by the necessity to get the pony into his stable cool and dry. It is the sweating, excitable pony that will cause most work at home if it arrives in that state. Once you have done the original cool-off for ten minutes or so, then jog on before you walk again. As a rule a hunter will signify when he requires to walk by gently beating his head up and down. Altering the length of your stirrup leathers also affords some relief, but slack riding is poor reward to a good pony, and now as much as ever it is incumbent on you to ride well. Even if your pony seems quite cool it is as well to let your girths right out and walk him for the final mile or so in order to prevent any likelihood of his breaking out into a sweat once he is home. In some cases it is even advisable to dismount and lead for the last mile or so. Your object, remember, is to bring into the stable a calm and cool pony. If it is raining keep walking and jogging on. A wet, cold, tired pony takes longer to dry than a wet, warm, tired pony.

On arrival home. Before entering the box, dismount, run up the irons and wash the pony's feet. A tub or bucket and water brush should be kept ready for this purpose. Do not wet above the coronet band. By placing your thumb in the heel prevent water running back into the heel. If raining do the feet in the box.

Lead into the box and at once remove the bridle before the pony rubs it on the manger. Do not tie up. Push the saddle back an inch or two or, if your pony likes a roll, remove the saddle altogether. Do not leave a cold wet saddle on the pony's back for long. Then place a rug, inside-out, over the loins and quarters. Stand back, close the door and leave the pony alone to stale but if he does not, then encourage him to do so by whistling or shaking some straw under him. Stay and watch in case the pony gets down to roll with the loose saddle on his back or turns round to look after you expecting his drink and so does not stale.

Next, mix luke-warm water with the gruel and take it to the pony, in his bucket. While he drinks fetch a small hay feed. If not already done, remove your coat etc., and be ready to wipe him over.

Give the hay feed. Remove the saddle and take it to a place of safety where it will air and dry. Smack the saddle region of the back smartly with the palm of the hand to restore circulation and to dry off the skin. Dry the sweat marks, by wiping the pony down with handfuls of straw. Then put the night rug on inside out and fasten. If the pony is still wet place straw on the back under the rug, or better still an open mesh "anti-sweat" rug. Dry off the heels with a rubber, and if the legs are wet and muddy wrap them in straw with stable bandages put on loosely. Some use ready warmed wool bandages for this purpose.

Now give him his corn, refill his bucket and go off to your meal. The purpose of the small hay feed on first arrival home is to get the tired pony's digestion into working order before it has the more concentrated feed thrust upon it. In some cases the corn feed may even be withheld until the final stable hour, but a good doer will undoubtedly accept concentrated feeds at both times.

Later, the same evening. Return to the pony and do only that which is necessary as regards cleaning and drying. It is rest that the pony now needs. In extreme cases, where the pony has "broken out" badly, it will be necessary to rug him up and walk him out. In any case all that is necessary is to make sure that he is dry, especially ears, throat, chest, back and loins. If these parts are damp, dry them with a rubber. Run your hands over his face, chest and legs, feeling for thorns, and under his belly to see that the worst of the mud is off. Remember, mud must only be brushed off when it is dry, never washed off.

Now, if satisfied that the pony is dry, passably clean and not in need of any "first aid", put on the blanket (if used) and the rug and unplait the mane. Water, hay-up, adjust bedding, refill bucket, and finally feed. Some people feed a bran mash or pudding (a mash with boiled oats or barley) after hunting because it is more easily digested.

Regulate ventilation, make sure of the door fastenings, turn out the lights and then for the saddlery!

The day after. Trot the pony up to see that no lameness has resulted from the previous day's activities.

Run the hand over the saddle and girth regions to make sure that no saddle injuries are in evidence.

Groom very thoroughly, paying extra attention to shoeing, and be especially on the look-out for girth galls, bumps, thorns and bruises, etc.

Avoid exercise, other than leading out in hand to take off stiffness and the filling out of the legs.

Increase the corn feed to compensate for energy expended the previous day. Make sure the pony can rest and lie down and has a good deep bed.

THE UNCLIPPED PONY KEPT OUT

This pony is living in a natural state "at grass" and in this case we have to consider only what we should do in order to compensate nature for any unnatural demands that we make upon the pony.

The evening before. The thick, greasy, natural coat is impossible to dry by rubbing and it is also very unpleasant to sit on when it is soaking wet. So, if it is wet, catch up the pony the evening before, pick out the feet, and stable in deep bedding to prevent draught around the pony's heels and legs. Hay-up, leave water in the box, and leave the top half of the stable door open because he is used to lots of fresh air. If a corn feed is used, give this at the same time as the hay.

Early morning. If the pony has been caught in over night, look round him, replenish water, hay-up, pick out feet and muck-out. Brush out mane and tail with body brush and lay with water brush. If the tail has been "pulled" (this is not recommended on a pony at grass), put on a tail bandage. Brush off mud and put the coat straight with the dandy brush. As stated elsewhere, nature provides a greasy substance in the coat which is the natural protection against wet and cold. We do not wish to remove this protection, therefore body brush grooming is wrong, and in any case, ineffective. If the pony normally receives a corn feed, then feed him, leave him tied up and break off for breakfast.

Should the pony not have been caught up over night, it will be necessary to fetch him from the field, wash out his feet, unless it is very cold when it is better just to use the hoof pick. Tie up under cover and proceed as above. If the pony is very wet and muddy any attempt to brush over will be useless. If only slightly damp it will be as well to leave the dandy brush work until after breakfast.

The start and arrival. There is little difference in procedure with the unclipped pony and the clipped pony. If the pony was too wet and muddy "to quarter" properly earlier, it may be possible to get some result now. The unclipped pony will inevitably sweat going on to the destination unless a quite impracticable slow pace is maintained. Steadier progress than with the clipped pony is thus essential, and 4 to 5 miles an hour is a fair estimate. The adjustment of the girths will need attention two or three times in the first half-hour.

On arrival. The paragraph for the corn-fed pony applies generally, but due consideration must be given to the fact that there is more strain on the lungs in fast work in an unclipped pony and care must be practised not to "burst" the pony excessively. Excessive sweating due to the long coat, will undoubtedly cause the pony to lose flesh, but nature's grease will counteract "chilling" so one need not be unduly alarmed, and need only take reasonable precautions on this account.

The road home. All that applies to the clipped pony applies here, but if the unclipped pony has sweated profusely, the long coat is unlikely to dry completely on the road home. The object to aim at is to arrive home with the pony reasonably cool under the long damp coat.

On arrival home. Dismount, remove bridle and saddle and put on a halter. Examine carefully feet and body to make sure that all is well. A draughty stable is a menace, so put the pony back into the field, even if he is sweating. If there are other ponies in the field, that are not being fed, then tie up, water and feed before turning out. Otherwise turn out straight away and feed and hay-up in the field.

The day after. Catch up on a halter and inspect for lameness, bruises, faulty shoes, etc. The thorough removal of sweat marks from the saddle region is important.

A pony clipped trace high will take less out of itself, by not sweating unduly, thus keeping in fitter condition. Also it will dry off much more quickly. During the winter ponies clipped trace high can be kept at grass provided the clip is not exaggerated by too much coat having been removed.

VETERINARY NOTES
THE MEDICINE CABINET

In a well organised stable a place should be set aside for the storage of first aid drugs and dressings to that they may be kept clean and free of dust and be quickly to hand when an emergency arises. The following is a suggested list of contents:—

A veterinary clinical thermometer. A pair of 4 in. blunt pointed surgical scissors. Calico bandages 2 in. and 3 in. sizes. Several 2 oz. rolls of cotton wool (small rolls are preferable to large 1 lb. packets, the unused portions of which once opened become soiled and unfit for future use). A few 1 oz. packets of lint. A roll of gamgee tissue. Small packets of oiled silk or mackintosh. Two colic drinks from your own veterinary surgeon. A pint bottle of lead lotion. A bottle of veterinary embrocation. A bottle of witch-hazel lotion. A 1 lb. tin of kaolin paste. A jar of cough electuary. A tin or "puffer" of antibiotic dusting powder. A jar of common salt, salt tablets or Epsom salts. A bottle of glycerine.

Do not attempt to use the thermometer without adult assistance.

FIRST AID

Wound dressing. Procedure has been revolutionised by the introduction of antibiotics. The use of antiseptics and disinfectants is today undesirable in that not only do they cause damage to the injured parts but also that they are antagonistic to the action of antibiotics. Cleansing with a saline solution followed by the application of an antibiotic in one or other form is the modern procedure.

Poulticing. A mixture of Epsom salts made into a paste with glycerine is simple and efficient. Kaolin paste is a most valuable application in all cases of bruising, abscess formation, swelling and pain. To use, ease the lid of the tin, stand in a saucepan half full of water and boil for five minutes. Test the temperature of the paste on the back of the hand before applying to the injured part. Lay on thick using an old blunt kitchen knife for the purpose. Cover with lint or cotton wool. Wrap a sheet of oiled silk or mackintosh over the dressing and bandage loosely with a woollen stable bandage. Renew after twenty-four hours.

Fomentation. This is a useful line of treatment where pain and swelling are in evidence, viz. septic wounds, sprains, contusions.

A piece of old blanket or towelling answers well provided it is clean. A square about 24 in. by 30 in. is required. Fold four-fold and hold by two of the corners. Immerse in a bucket of warm water to which salt, one handful to a half bucket of water, has been added. Lift out and wrap round the injured part. Re-immerse and re-apply. Bring the temperature of the water up when necessary by adding more warm water from a kettle. Continue for twenty minutes. In severe cases fomentation may be repeated two or three times a day until relief is obtained.

Tubbing. Useful for all injuries of the lower part of the limb and of the foot region. A wooden bucket is best; failing that a rubber or plastic bucket or a feed tin. Half fill with warm water to which salt has been added. Pick out the foot, scrub it clean from a second bucket of water and then immerse it gently into the wooden bucket. Splash about with the hand and add more warm water from time to time. In doing this one hand must be kept constantly in the bucket to test the temperature. Continue for twenty minutes and repeat twice daily in cases of severe injury.

Hose-piping. The use of a continuous stream of cold water is a simple and valuable form of treatment in a variety of conditions, viz. in cleaning up a wound, in reducing the pain and swelling resulting from a sprain, etc. Hose-piping should not be resorted to with cracked heels, nor in frosty weather. Heels should be packed with vaseline and dried afterwards.

In default of a piped supply of water a stirrup pump and bucket of cold water answers almost as well. Commence with a slow gentle stream of water and apply first of all to the hoof. Work gradually up the leg until the injured part is reached. Increase pressure gradually. Continue for twenty minutes and repeat twice a day in severe cases.

Steaming a head. Useful in cases of excessive discharge from the nostrils, viz. nasal catarrh.

Place a handful of soft hay in the bottom of a canvas or improvised nosebag or a bucket. Add a teaspoonful of friars balsam or cucalyptus oil. Pour in half a pint of boiling water. Swing the bag for a minute or two and then place on the horse's muzzle. Allow the pony to inhale. As a rule little resistance is offered. Continue for five minutes, remove, add more hot water and repeat. Steaming the head should be limited to two occasions in a week only. In cases of pneumonia it is best to use a bucket and not to exclude the air, and it can then be continued for a longer period and more frequently.

As the interior of the bag will be heavily infected after use the contents should be burnt and the bag turned inside-out and scalded on each occasion.

ADMINISTRATION OF MEDICINE

In the feed. The simplest way but useless if the pony is so ill that he is off his feed. The feed should be damped first and the powder or mixture added to it. Offer when the pony is hungry.

In the drinking water. Useful provided the medicine will mix with the water and the horse will drink it.

On the tongue. For this purpose the medicine is supplied made into a stiff paste with treacle, then known as electuary. This is smeared on the tongue or the back teeth. A smooth blunt stick is necessary for the purpose. A wooden kitchen spoon with the sides of the bowl sawn off leaving a width of about $1\frac{1}{2}$ in. answers well.

Horse drinks. To drench a horse raise the head and administer slowly from the bottle. When one mouthful has been swallowed give another. To raise a pony's head, untie the headrope, fasten to the middle-front of the nose-band and pass the free end over a beam. If the pony coughs lower the head immediately.

Other methods. Veterinary surgeons also employ the following: Dosing by the stomach tube:— This is passed through the nostril, throat and on down into the stomach. The medicine is poured in by gravity. The advantages are that no waste results and that the horse tastes nothing. Dosing by hypodermic syringe:— The injection of the drug is made beneath the skin, into a muscle or into a vein.

NURSING

The owner of a well-loved pony will always wish to do the best if the pony is ill or in pain and likewise what is right and proper in such cases.

A sick, lame or injured pony should be made as comfortable as circumstances permit and kept out of reach, but not necessarily out of sight, of stable companions. A loose box or a special paddock should be provided. Special gentleness in handling is an obvious consideration.

Wounds. In dealing with exposed wounds avoid sweeping, shaking-up bedding or in any other way raising a dust. Indeed, bedding may with advantage be lightly damped down. Peat moss and sawdust are bad forms of bedding in such cases. Do not get alarmed if wounds are left uncovered or unbandaged. It is nature's way in the horse and most wounds progress better if they are exposed to the air. In cases in which wounds are bandaged, and this applies as a rule to wounds of the legs only, remember that the leg may swell under the bandage causing great pain. Therefore watch for swelling and make a rule to remove every bandage every day and replace. Never use safety pins. Wash hands before dressing a wound and again afterwards. Keep all dressings as clean as possible and burn all that are soiled.

Lameness. This calls for the exercise of much common sense. If the pony will lie down, then provide a good bed. If he will not lie, then reduce the bedding so that it does not become tangled around his feet through his inability to move freely. Here again, if bandages are in use, make quite sure that they are not too tight. Concentrated feeds must be reduced in a horse thrown out of work by lameness and laxative diet substituted. With the single exception of certain nerve injuries rest is essential to recovery.

Illness. If the pony has a high temperature there is quite a lot that the good nurse can do to help. Clothing will be necessary and stable bandages are an additional comfort. These should be removed and replaced once daily. Since the pony will be feeling very ill, the less he is fussed the better. Grooming should be dispensed with altogether or reduced to a simple wipe over with a damp rubber. If a second box is available it is a good plan to prepare and move him into it. The soiled box can then be mucked out without disturbing the patient. Gentle sponging of eyes and nostrils is refreshing. Rubbing the legs and fetlocks with the palms of the hands when bandages are off restores circulation. Earpulling, that is to say, grasping the ears at the poll and allowing them to slip gently through the closed hand, is comforting.

Water is important in these cases and an ample clean fresh supply should always be available to the pony and it ought to be changed several times a day. Ponies do not like warm water.

Ventilation calls for attention but there is no illness of the pony in which fresh air is wrong. A draught is another matter.

The fact that a sick pony refuses his feed is always a source of great worry to the owner. Nature however knows best and the time to get busy in the matter is when the pony is a little better and

226 MANUAL OF HORSEMANSHIP

inclined to feed once again. Fresh green grass is then usually more acceptable than anything else, as also sliced apple and carrots. Feed very little at a time and offer it often. Never leave a heap of stale feed in front of a sick horse. Milk, offered from a bucket is a good pick-me-up but not all ponies like milk. Bran mashes are normally the staple diet for a sick horse so put in a supply of bran and learn how to make a bran mash properly (*see page* 184).

It is an excellent plan in these cases to keep the temperature record in the form of a chart. All that is necessary is a sheet of square-ruled paper and four drawing pins to fasten it to the wall. Such a chart speaks louder than words and will show at a glance just how the pony is progressing day by day.

Eye injuries. In dealing with injuries of the eye, stable the pony in a darkened box. Do not put on eye shades which only collect tears and with them dirt.

Finally if your veterinary surgeon is due to pay you a visit see that the pony is caught up and ready for him. Have a jug of warm water, bowl, towel and soap ready for his use. At each visit obtain fresh instructions regarding (1) feeding, (2) exercise and (3) treatment and then follow them carefully.

WOUNDS

Wounds are a common cause of disability in ponies. Small ponies are probably more commonly placed on the sick list for this reason than for any other.

Four types of wound are recognised.

Clean cut, such as are caused by a sharp instrument, i.e. a knife or piece of glass. They are not very common.

Torn wounds, a tear of the skin or flesh caused, as for example, by barbed wire or a projecting nail. Common.

Punctured wounds, caused by penetrating thorns, stakes, nails, etc. The entrance is small but penetration may be deep. They are always serious and particularly so if in the vicinity of a joint.

Bruised wounds, caused by kicks, blows, falls, galls, over-reaching, etc. Relatively common.

Treatment of wounds

This falls into four stages:—

Stage 1. Arrest the bleeding. If only small vessels are involved bleeding generally ceases of its own accord within twenty minutes. Bleeding is always a worry to the owner but rarely a danger to the horse and in any case must be regarded as nature's method of washing out a wound. Excessive bleeding on the other hand, such as the spurting of bright red blood from a severed artery, calls for control, which should be attempted either by tight bandaging of the wound itself, or better still, by applying pressure above the wound, i.e. on the side nearest to the heart. The hunting stock removed and used as a bandage or a pebble placed inside a hand-kerchief and tied on to the leg is the hunting field emergency measure for doing this. It may be necessary to ligature the severed artery, in which case veterinary advice should be sought.

Stage 2. Clean up. This is by far the most important part. The time and energy expended in the preliminary cleansing of a wound is four times as valuable as anything of a similar nature done later. Many a wound can be caused to heal quickly and well through a thorough preliminary cleansing.

Clip the hair from the skin in the vicinity first of all and then wash. The simplest and most efficient method is to hosepipe, i.e. to trickle a continuous stream of water on to the wound for twenty minutes (*see page* 222). Do this very gently as the injury will be painful. In default of this soap and water, or salt and water, may be used but the employment of sponges and disinfectants is to be avoided.

Stage 3. Dress. If small, the wound should then be liberally covered by dusting with an antibiotic powder preferably applied from a puffer. If extensive, the wound should be packed with a paste of freshly prepared Epsom salt in glycerine and then covered with a piece of oiled silk or mackintosh.

Stage 4. Protection, i.e. bandaging. This is not always necessary and in any case is normally only possible on the lower parts of the limbs. Cover the wound with lint or gauze-covered cotton wool and bandage lightly to allow room for subsequent swelling should such occur.

Additional measures. Stop oats and put the pony on to mashes or green food instead. Avoid raising a dust by sweeping or opening out hay or bedding when a wound is exposed. Where swelling is excessive resort may be had to fomentation or tubbing (*see page* 222). An injection for the prevention of lockjaw should be given unless the horse is protected for life against this disease. This is especially necessary with deep-punctured wounds in districts where lockjaw is prevalent (*see page* 242).

Subsequent dressings. Repeat stages 3 and 4 daily and if the wound is dirty, then stage 2 also. It is generally possible to know within a few days whether a wound is healing well or otherwise. Adverse signs are an increase in lameness and swelling of the part, particularly the swelling that creeps up the limb, signs of sweating or going off feed. In all such cases professional advice should then be sought without delay.

Sewing up. As a general rule the larger a wound the better chance there is that it will do well. It is the small punctured wound that is dangerous, especially those near a joint or a tendon sheath. The question whether a wound should be sutured or not is best left to the veterinary surgeon.

Antibiotics. The introduction of antibiotic drugs such as penicillin, streptomycin, etc. has completely revolutionised all previous ideas on the treatment of wounds. Their action is to kill or inhibit the multiplication of germs within the wound which they are capable of doing to a remarkable degree. So much so that today the employment of disinfectants has been completely superseded. Antibiotic treatment ought always to be instituted in cases of punctured wounds in the vicinity of joints, into tendon sheaths or in the region of the foot. Recovery time is thereby shortened and crippling after effects avoided.

Common wounds

The following are among the more common forms of injury with which horsemen are required to deal.

Bit injuries, which show on the bars of the mouth, on the tongue, cheeks or in the chin groove. Due to badly-fitting or worn bits, or rough riding and to ragged molar teeth.

Discontinue work for a few days. Wash out the mouth with warm salt and water after feeding. Adjust or change the bit. Mouth injuries are notoriously quick in healing.

Girth galls, which show on the soft skin behind the elbow. They are due to soft condition of the pony, too hard, too tight, too loose or too broad a girth. It is best not to use a saddle for a few days, then subsitute a Balding or a string girth for that in use, or encase the girth in a clean length of motor car wheel inner tube. A pad of lambs wool beneath the girth relieves pressure and pain at the injured spot.

The skin may be hardened and recovery hastened by application of salt and water, methylated spirit or witch hazel lotion to the part. In severe cases the application of a cortisone ointment considerably reduces inflammation.

Where the skin is unbroken dab several times a day with witch hazel lotion.

Saddle galls and sore backs. These terms cover any saddle injury from a slight rub to a severe swelling or abrasion. The cause is the same in all cases, viz. friction or pressure. The reasons, however, are many, among which may be named badly-fitting saddles which pinch the withers, saddles overdue for re-stuffing, broken saddle tree, bad riding, and impedimenta hung on to the saddle.

Stop work. The pony may, with advantage, be exercised in hand. Dress open wounds by fomentation or the application of kaolin paste for a few days (*see page* 222). Later, harden off with salt and water or methylated spirit. Trace and remove the cause of the injury.

With partly healed wounds the pony may be returned to work by using a numnah pad beneath the saddle in which a hole has been cut to accommodate the injury and relieve pressure on the part (*see page* 100).

Broken knees. This term is reserved to the condition resulting when a pony stumbles, falls and injures the surface of one or both knees. The injury varies from a slight abrasion of the skin to actual exposure of the knee bones.

Treat by hose-piping (*see page* 222) three or four times a day and continue for as long a period at a time as possible. Kaolin poultices are useful in severe cases. Protection of the wound may be afforded and retention of the kaolin paste in position by placing on the leg a knee-cap lined with clean lint. On no account bandage the knee as a bandage may become painfully tight through slipping down or from swelling of the part. Veterinary advice should be obtained when the injury is more than skin deep.

Brushing wounds, caused by the pony striking the opposite leg generally on the inner aspect of the fetlock but sometimes the coronet. The reasons are many, as for example, bad conformation, bad action, a prominent clench, heavy shoes, ill-fitting shoes, youth, old age, overwork, underfeeding.

Trace the cause. Adjust the shoeing and fit a feather-edge or other suitable shoe (see page 208). In extreme cases the use of a brushing boot on the injured leg becomes a necessity.

Treads are wounds of the coronet region either self-inflicted or caused by another pony placing his shod foot on his neighbour's coronet. Treat as for a bruised wound or rub daily for a few days.

Over-reaches are self-inflicted wounds of the fore tendons or bulbs of the heels, due to interference by the toe of the hind foot. Normally, the injury results at a gallop or when jumping. The wound is either entirely accidental or due to faulty shoeing behind or faulty action (see also page 207). Treat as for a bruised wound. Examine the hind foot. There should be no toe clip present on the hind shoe of a fast-moving pony (see also pages 207 and 208).

Bruised sole is a true bruise and generally results from picking up a stone in the foot. Some ponies have naturally thin soles and in consequence are liable to bruising on any flinty track. Shoe up with a leather sole.

Pricked foot and under-run sole. These are penetrating wounds of the foot and though due to different causes may be considered together. The former arises through the accidental driving of a shoeing nail into the sensitive structure of the foot during shoeing. The latter results from the penetration of the sole by a sharp object such as a nail, sharp flint, or piece of tin or glass.

These wounds are generally troublesome as they are of a dangerous type, i.e. with a small opening and deep penetration. Festering may result in a day or two, when intense pain is shown. Such injuries call for professional attention, particularly as there is always the attendant risk of lockjaw.

Rope galls are abrasions of the skin behind the pastern or knee. They are due to a leg over a rope or chain, as when a horse is tied up too long. Apply kaolin paste and thereafter treat with dry boracic powder and a bandage.

Cracked heels, i.e. chapping of the skin behind the pastern. It results from exposure to wet conditions or neglect following washing of the legs. Lameness may be severe. In all cases treat first of all with pads of cotton wool soaked in lead lotion and bandaged on. Thereafter dry off with boracic powder.

LAMENESS

Lameness is the commonest form of disability in the horse (as distinct from the pony) and every horseman should have some understanding of the subject, though, for the most part, it is a job for the expert.

When faced with the problem of a lame horse or pony it is first necessary to discover in which leg he is lame, and following that, to ascertain the part of the limb concerned.

To find the right leg. The pony should be trotted up in hand at as slow a pace as possible. Rising ground is a help so that the pony moves slightly down hill on the return.

When a pony is lame in a foreleg he will nod his head each time the *sound* leg comes to the ground. If he is lame behind, the weight will similarly be seen to fall on the *sound* limb when it comes to the ground.

To find the part of the leg. Three things must be searched for, viz. heat, pain and swelling. All three may not necessarily be in evidence and in any case swelling will not be shown in the foot since it cannot expand. In some cases only one of these indications will be present, and in obscure cases of lameness, none at all.

Ninety per cent of all lameness being centred in the foot, begin the examination there. The chance of the seat of trouble being elsewhere becomes progressively less the further one travels up the leg. Throughout the examination a constant comparison with the opposite leg should be made, particularly in relation to differences in heat.

The following are some of the commoner forms of lameness in the horse. Reference should be made to Figures 62(a) and (b) given on pages 234 and 235.

Stone in the foot. Occurs suddenly while at work, more particularly on a flinty road. Dismount and pick up the foot. A stone is lodged between shoe and frog. Remove the stone and if lameness persists walk the pony home on grass.

Bruised sole. Caused in a similar manner. The sole is tender on pressure and may show a red mark. Treat as indicated on page 231.

Nail binding, due to a shoeing nail pressing on the sensitive parts of the foot. Shows within a day or two of being reshod. Remove the offending nail and the pony will go sound (*see page* 204).

Pricked foot, where a shoeing nail has actually penetrated the sensitive parts of the foot. Associated with a visit to the forge and shows on leaving. Treat as indicated on page 222 under "tubbing", but see also the advice given on page 231 regarding this type of injury.

Corns are bruises of the sole in the heel region just beneath the heels of the shoe. Caused by bad-fitting shoes and neglect to have the pony re-shod when due. May be a simple bruise or in severe cases actually festering. Remove shoe, tub foot and re-shoe with a three-quarter length shoe.

Laminitis or "Fever in the feet" is a condition of sudden intense inflammation of the sensitive structures which line the inside of the wall of the foot. Both forefeet or all four feet are affected at the same time but never a single foot. It is one of the most painful conditions from which a pony can suffer because the foot cannot expand to accommodate the acute swelling within. Causes are various but two common ones are excessive feeding and fast trotting on hard roads. The disease frequently occurs in grossly fat children's ponies with access to lush grass in May. The affected

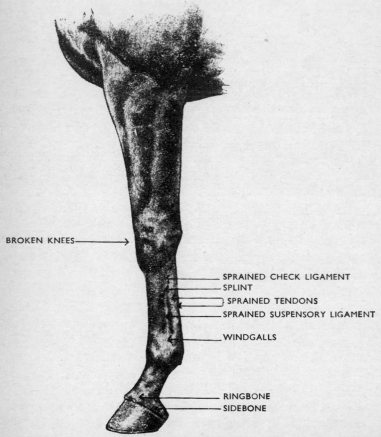

BROKEN KNEES ———————→

SPRAINED CHECK LIGAMENT
SPLINT
} SPRAINED TENDONS
SPRAINED SUSPENSORY LIGAMENT

WINDGALLS

RINGBONE
SIDEBONE

FIGURE 62.   SEATS OF LAMENESS
(a)   The Foreleg

pony stands on the heels with the feet thrust forward and can only be moved with difficulty or not at all. Severe cases call for professional attention.

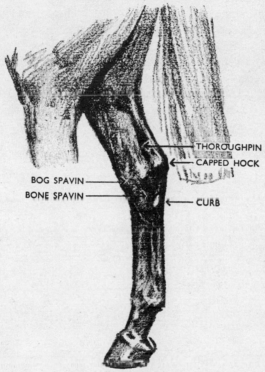

FIGURE 62. SEATS OF LAMENESS
(b) Inner aspect of Hind leg

First-aids in treatment are to remove the shoes, cut down the feet drastically and give forced exercise on grass or a tarred road (not on a flinty road) several times a day. This will be painful at first but it is essential if circulation of blood within the foot is to be restored. The feed must be reduced. The pony should have cold application applied to the feet as by hose-piping, standing in mud or best of all in a stream of running water where he may be tied to a tree. Modern treatment consists in the early injection of an anti-histamine or a cortisone drug the relief afforded by which is sometimes spectacular, and goes far to check the after effects of permanent disability, shifting of the coffin bone or dropped sole. When improvement is shown the pony should be exercised, shod with a special surgical shoe and turned out to graze on poor land where he cannot get much to eat and will be constantly on the move to find it, or grazing limited to an hour or two only each day.

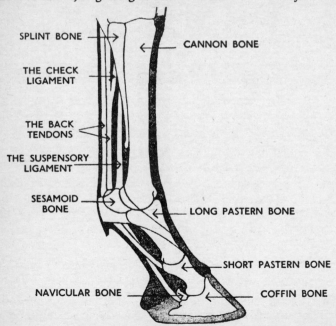

FIGURE 63.   SECTION OF FORELEG
Showing parts liable to injury

Ringbones are bony enlargements of the pastern bones either "low"—on the coronet, or "high"—above the coronet. Both forms are slow forming and call for special treatment. The more serious are those which involve a joint.

Sidebones form in the heel region, as a result of which the flexibility of the heels is lost.

Thrush is a foul condition of the cleft of the frog due to neglect. Clean out daily and dust with boracic powder or other dry dressing.

Sprained fetlock joint in which the whole joint is swollen and painful. It results from a twist, as for example, in putting a foot into a rabbit hole. Pack up with kaolin paste, renewing daily, for three days, and thereafter treat with pads of cotton wool soaked in lead lotion, or by hose-piping the leg.

Windgall is a swelling of joint sacs just above and to the sides of the fetlock joint. Often painful and associated with lameness when first formed, but later generally gives little trouble. Treat with kaolin paste followed, after three days, with lead lotion bandages.

Sprained tendons, including sprains of the check ligament and suspensory ligament, all of which are located behind the cannon bone (*see figure* 63). Any one of these may show injury due to strain. Heat, pain and swelling will all be in evidence. Treat in the first place with kaolin paste for three days, and follow up with cotton wool pads soaked in lead lotion or frequent hose-piping. Sometimes injuries to these structures are too severe to clear up with simple first aid. If swelling and lameness persist professional advice should be sought.

Splints are small bony knobs which form on the splint bone, the cannon bone or both. They are troublesome while forming but later may cause little inconvenience unless they involve the knee joint or press on the suspensory ligament. Lameness from this cause is rare after six years of age. It may be necessary to apply a blister or treat with a cortisone injection.

Bone spavin is a bony enlargement on the lower aspect of the inside of the hock. Lameness from this cause is peculiar in that although the pony moves off lame, the lameness disappears in about five minutes. The condition calls for special treatment.

Bog spavin is a soft swelling of the hock joint which shows to the front of the inner side. Due to strain. Treat by fomentation and massage.

Curb is a sprain of the ligament or tendon a short way below the point of the hock which then appears "bowed". Due to sudden strain. Treat with kaolin paste.

Thoroughpin is a soft swelling in front of the point of the hock which sometimes can be pushed through from one side of the leg to the other. Due to strain. Treat by massage.

SOME COMMON AILMENTS

Colic

Colic (pain in the belly) "the disease to which equine flesh is heir", may be met with anywhere and at any time. The indications are unmistakable and once seen never forgotten. There is general uneasiness, the horse is off his feed, restlessness, looking round at the flanks, kicking at the belly and getting up and down and rolling. Causes are irregularities in feeding, sudden changes of diet, chronic indigestion, sand in the drinking water (as when watering from a shallow river bed) and many other conditions.

The horse should be given a colic drink, preferably one from your own veterinary surgeon, which should always be available for emergency use. Move the pony to a safe place so that he cannot become cast in his box or stall when down and rolling. Better still walk him slowly round and round a field if weather permits. Throw a light rug over when doing this. Colic cases are often safest loose in a field provided there is no ditch into which they can become cast.

Some colic cases are of short duration, i.e. lasting less than two hours. If relief does not take place within this time or if the pony becomes violent, it must be assumed that the case is a serious one requiring professional assistance without further delay.

Simple fever

By fever is understood a rise in body temperature as revealed by the use of the thermometer. Temperature taking should always be resorted to whenever a horse is found off colour as for example refusing his feed, dull, listless, showing a staring coat, quickened breathing or shivering. Normal in the horse is 100·5°. A slight rise of, say, 1 degree above this may be of little consequence. A rise to 103° or more however indicates that something is seriously wrong and calls for energetic action.

Feverish conditions occur either because the body is being subjected to invading germs or to a nervous reaction to pain. Fortunately today the use of antibiotic drugs enables us to check the invading germs before they can cause real harm, e.g. a pleurisy or pneumonia. Professional aid ought therefore to be sought without delay and in most cases speedy recovery will result if antibiotic treatment is instituted early. For the general care of the horse (see page 225).

Cold in the head

This shows as a yellow or white discharge from both nostrils which is sometimes profuse and soils the manger, edges of the door and the ground outside. Simple catarrh often develops as a result of lack of fresh air as for example after confinement to a stuffy horse box on a long journey and it may even appear when a horse, up from grass, is stabled once again.

Isolate. Stop work. Arrange for plenty of fresh air in the stable but not a draught. Rug up and put on bandages. Feed off the ground to allow the nostrils to drain. Supply a separate watering bucket. Dispense with the use of sponges. Clear the nostrils three times a day with cotton wool which must be burnt afterwards. Feed bran mashes. Steam the head (*see page* 223). Take the horse's temperature and if it is above 103° send for professional assistance.

Strangles

This is a contagious disease, mainly of young horses, but it may also be seen in older animals that have escaped an attack in youth. It is always preceded by a sharp rise of temperature which may be as high as 105°. Thereafter the typical signs of the disease develop but to varying degrees in different animals, namely a profuse nasal catarrh with abscess formation in the jowl region. The horse is greatly distressed, off feed, swallowing is difficult, the throat region enlarged and tense. In due course the abscess between the jaw bones bursts and drains following which there is immediate relief.

Isolate and provide for strictly separate watering and feeding utensils. Give attention to the rules of good nursing as indicated at page 225. A peculiarity of the disease is that in the majority of cases the final results are better if it is allowed to run its course unchecked as by the use of antibiotics. Treatment should aim at the good care and nursing of the sick animal and the hastening of the development and bursting of the jowl abscess. Some promote this by fomenting the throat region. A frightening illness but rarely a dangerous one.

Simple cough

Laryngitis or sore throat. There are several different kinds of cough in the horse and all of them call for treatment necessitating the horse being taken out of work. High feeding should be reduced and a soft diet substituted which can be swallowed without discomfort, damped down to lay dust or even sprinkled with treacle. Bran mashes and green food are particularly indicated. If hay is fed immerse the net in the horse trough before feeding to soften the hay. Better still play a kettle of boiling water over it. Avoid raising a dust in the stable. The throat should be rubbed twice daily from ear to ear with a mild liniment using the back of the hand for the purpose. Small doses of a good cough electuary should be placed on the tongue or the back teeth two or three times a day (*see page* 223).

Equine influenza

This term is used today for a contagious virus infection of horses which takes the form of a coughing epidemic. Though a mild disease it plays havoc with the sporting and other fixtures for which horses are required. Actually two viruses are concerned, an European and an American, and unfortunately an attack by one gives no protection against a subsequent attack by the other.

There is an initial rise of temperature which in some cases may be as high as 106° but it is of short duration and may be missed. This is followed by the onset of coughing which at first is dry and shallow but later becomes more fluid and soft. Duration varies greatly but averages about 10 days. The disease is highly contagious and spreads rapidly throughout the stable. Work must be stopped or a simple illness may become a serious one. Treatment is on the general lines for simple cough given above but the condition shows an annoying tendency to run its own course irrespective of efforts made to alleviate matters.

It is now possible for horses to be given a protective injection against these two viruses which covers them for one year. It should be renewed at yearly intervals. It is recommended that this always be done before the commencement of the show season.

Lockjaw

Tetanus. This is a serious disease in the horse. It is due to a germ which lives in the soil and which gains access to the body as a result of a wound. The disease develops about ten days later. Stiffness in gait and shooting of the third eyelid across the eye characterise the condition. Immediate and drastic treatment is essential if the horse is to be saved.

Prevention, however, is better than cure and fortunately two methods are now available. The first consists in the early injection of a dose of lockjaw serum whenever a horse sustains a wound. This will safeguard him against the development of the germ within his body during the next ten days. The other method is to have the horse protected for life by the injection of doses of tetanus toxoid. Horse owners are advised to have all new purchases protected for life in this way so that worries about this dreadful disease are at an end.

Broken wind

This is a chronic and incurable disease of the lungs characterised by a persistent cough and heaving of the flanks, distress in movement and inability to perform fast work. The condition is very common in small ponies. It results from a tear of the lung structure, the moulds in dusty hay and straw being considered nowadays a prime cause. The cough which characterises this disease is deep, hollow and "graveyard" appearing to come from the belly region. There is a double movement of the flank in breathing. Given time and rest a considerable measure of repair may set in, the cough becoming less marked and less frequent. The important points in treatment are to run the pony at grass as far as is possible, damp all feeds particularly the hay feed and to avoid any kind of dusty fodder.

Azoturia

This peculiar disease of horses may be met with in any type of animal at any season of the year. It shows as a sudden breakdown of fibres in the big muscles of the loins and quarters and is associated with strong muscular exertion following a period of rest on a full working diet. Hence the name "Monday morning disease" and the practice of mashing down working horses on a Saturday night. The cause is unknown. While at work, particularly fast work, onset is marked by a slackening of the pace and muscular stiffness. If the horse is pressed, conditions get worse until he comes to a standstill and may even stagger, sway or fall. Blowing, distress and sweating may be in evidence. Examination of the quarters reveals that the muscles there are hardened and tense (termed "boarded") with muscular tremors.

The rider should dismount, slacken girth, remove jacket and throw it over the loins. The horse should be allowed to rest in a sheltered position. When able to move he should be taken home in a trailer or failing that stabled in a nearby stable, shed or barn. Rug up, keep warm, make comfortable. Allow plenty of drinking water and feed a laxative diet. Massage the affected muscles or apply hot packs or an electric blanket pending the arrival of the veterinary surgeon. Do not hasten back into work for four or five days. Recurrence is likely in horses that have once shown an attack.

Roaring and whistling

These are abnormal noises made by a horse when moving at a fast pace and result from a paralysis of one of the nerves of the throat. The former is an exaggerated form of the latter. Both conditions are extremely rare in ponies. The treatment is surgical.

SKIN DISEASES

Lice infection, probably the commonest skin condition of the pony. It is seen more particularly in the long-coated animal at grass about the month of February. The affected animal rubs the crest and tail and the hair comes away, leaving smooth bare patches. Treatment is easy, namely to powder the pony liberally from poll to croup along the middle line of the back with a special agricultural lice powder (not the horticultural kind intended for plants). Repeat every few days. To get rid of the eggs or nits clip the horse and run over lightly with a singeing lamp.

Sweet itch, an irritable condition of the skin of the crest, withers and croup region, which appears in June and disappears about September. Fairly common in ponies in certain parts of the country. The affected animal rubs these areas raw often using an overhanging branch of a tree or bush for the purpose. This condition is now known to arise from the fact that the pony is allergic to some substance, generally one of the spring grasses. Train oil and sulphur, though messy, afford some relief. Stabling by day out of direct sunshine undoubtedly helps.

Ringworm of the horse or pony. It shows on the skin as round areas, the size of a florin, from which the hair pulls away in a complete circle. May occur on any part of the body. Painting daily with tincture of iodine may relieve the condition but some cases are more resistant. Isolate the pony. Stop grooming. Disinfect the rugs and grooming kit.

Pustular dermatitis, or contagious acne, a disease in which small round inflamed areas, varying in size from a sixpence to a half-penny, appear on various parts of the body, particularly the girth and saddle region. The hair comes away in circles leading to confusion of the disease with ringworm. The disease is infectious and is carried by stable dust, grooming kit and saddlery. Isolate the pony, stop grooming and exercise. Disinfect saddlery, grooming kit and rugs. Paint areas, as they appear, with tincture of iodine and repeat the painting three times.

Mange of the horse. This disease is controlled by the State and is now rare in the British Isles.

Warbles. These show as lumps beneath the skin of the back, usually in the saddle region and more commonly in spring time. The cause is the maggot of the warble-fly which in the course of a few days bores a small hole in the skin and pops out. Warbles are best left alone until the maggot has made its exit when a little wound powder or gall ointment may be applied to the hole. If interfered with in the course of development the maggot may be killed under the skin resulting in a permanent and troublesome thickening. Ponies should not be ridden when warbles are developing.

UNTHRIFTINESS
(Malnutrition)

This subject is of sufficient importance to warrant a section to itself. The horse that fails to maintain condition in spite of every care is a source of worry to the owner as also a matter of reproach among friends.

Condition. Horsemen employ an extensive vocabulary to describe the condition carried by a horse and much misuse of the terms is seen. In general these are:— Gross condition; in which the horse is overfat, excess being particularly notable in the crest and loin regions. Good condition; in which the body is well covered, the coat sleek and the horse possessing a general appearance of well-being. Light condition: which falls short of the preceding ideal. Poor condition: where the ribs are in evidence and the quarter muscles mean. Debilitated: where the general condition is below par and the horse unuseable. Emaciation: meaning skin and bone, an extreme rarely seen in Britain today.

Good condition. With careful management it is possible to keep a horse in good condition throughout the whole of the year whether under the natural conditions of liberty at grass supplemented by winter feeding, or the artificial conditions of hard keep stabled, as in a riding establishment. The objection to the above is that it is unnatural and because this is so duration of life is shortened. Most experienced horsemen prefer to subscribe to a system whereby the horse is worked hard for a season as a result of which condition is lost. This in turn is followed by a period of rest during which the lost condition is made good. This system is known as The Summering of Hunters and The Wintering of Polo Ponies. There are two main advantages: firstly this follows nature's intention in regard to the life cycle of the horse and secondly the working life of the horse is prolonged in that not only is the digestive system rested but also heart and limbs.

Other terms used by horsemen. A "Good Doer" is a horse which in spite of indifferent care and sometimes even neglect succeeds in maintaining good condition. Cobs are often good doers. A "Bad Doer" on the other hand is a horse which in spite of every care and attention never looks really well. They are expensive to keep and the explanation is generally elusive. A "Dainty Feeder" is a horse which is unusually fastidious in the matter of clearing up his feed. Such call for the exercise of great patience and ingenuity in overcoming the fault. In nearly all cases an explanation exists but it may take weeks or months of painstaking study and familiarity with the animal to arrive at the reason and to overcome it. Some horses, for example, will only feed at night, some only if a light is left in the stable, some only provided they are certain of not being molested by neighbours at feeding times.

Causes of Unthriftiness. These are as follows and they are of importance in the order given:—

Faulty watering arrangements. Nothing detracts so seriously from maintenance of condition in a horse as this, particularly water shortage.

Faulty feeding arrangements. The possibilities here are legion but perhaps the most common fault is the feeding of inferior quality forage. Stale, musty concentrates are not only unacceptable to a horse but actually harmful and in any case the nutritive value of such is low. The imperative need for adequate supplies of bulk in the feeding of the horse has been emphasised elsewhere in this book but the whole subject is greatly complicated today by modern methods of saving the hay crop whereby it is taken and baled too quickly and in semi-damp state. A sample of perfect hay today is indeed hard to come by and our horses suffer accordingly. The greatest care needs to be exercised when making purchases of hay so as to secure the very best procurable. Half the troubles in maintaining condition disappear if only a sweet nutritious hay feed can be offered. Irregular feeding hours, lack of rest periods in which to digest the feed, bullying by a stable companion at feeding times and many another such fault contribute to the detriment of condition.

Inadequate supplies of forage. It is almost impossible to kill a horse by overwork. Provided the quantity of forage offered is adequate to the work performed by the horse and the necessary time for feeding and rest are provided for, then condition should be maintained. Hence the rule to feed in proportion to the work done. The effect of overwork on the horse is "staleness" or "boredom" and not strictly "weariness" and stories of strings of overtired overworked horses leaving riding stables are not in accordance with fact.

Age. Age affects maintenance of condition. The crisis in the life of a horse shows at about 17 years of age when condition becomes more difficult to maintain and the working potential of the animal is reduced. Old horses suffer greatly from cold and special care is called for in winter time. Nevertheless it is a remarkable fact that many horses pass the crisis in life without showing any deterioration whatever beyond a gradual slowing of pace. Where this occurs the horse may well go forward and lead a useful life up to 25 years of age or even longer. Such is a certain guarantee that the animal suffers from no physical disability whatever.

Deficiency conditions. These may be mineral or vitamin. Few horses do well on land lacking lime. Soil licking, gnawing wood or bark and even dung eating are manifestations of a craving for mineral. Soil sampling is a simple answer here and for the most part is a free service to agriculture. A vitamin deficiency is now well established as a contributing cause to lack of condition and where it operates the injection of a dose of the vital element is often attended by a quite remarkable improvement in the condition carried by the animal.

Dental irregularities. Dental defects are often a contributing cause, and in some cases the direct cause of lack of condition, due to inability to masticate properly without pain. The grinding process carried out by the back (molar) teeth in the horse results in sharp edges developing upon them which lacerate the cheek or tongue. Such is readily corrected by the simple process known as teeth rasping. Other defects include broken or split teeth causing much pain. In general dental irregularities in the horse are easy of correction and horsemen are advised to have a teeth inspection made of their horses yearly or every other year from the age of eight years onwards.

Worms. All horses harbour worms. It is possible to eliminate them by suitable dosage but within a few days they are in evidence again. In general, in a healthy body and a well conditioned horse, worms are of little consequence because the resistance of the animal is sufficient to overcome them. It is in the weakened body that they exert their evil work. A vicious circle is set up whereby the multiplication of worms is at the same time the result of debilitation as also its cause. Deworming is then called for.

Many types of worm infest horses. The best known and most dangerous of these is the little red worm which makes its nests within the lining of the bowel thereby destroying its function and in extreme cases leading to scouring and emaciation. The inch long white stromgyle inhabits the blood stream as well as the bowel and is sometimes the direct cause of the blocking of blood vessels, aneurisms and strangulation. Seat or whip worms are made evident by a soiling of the dock region and are a contributing cause to malnutrition when present in excessive numbers.

It is possible to ascertain both the quantity and variety of worms infesting a horse by the simple process known as dung sampling. A small amount of droppings is submitted to laboratory tests whereby the number and type of worm eggs present reveals the degree and type of infection.

Each year, better and better worm drugs are discovered for use in the deworming of horses, not only more lethal against the worms themselves but less harmful to the horse. It is not advisable here to name the best worm medicine available for such is certain to be superseded eventually by a better preparation. Horse owners faced with a worming problem are advised to consult their veterinary surgeon for advice as to the latest and most potent preparation and the dosage.

Disease. Internal growths are a common cause of lack of condition in horses from 15 years of age onwards and this includes consumption. The last named condition should always be considered in a horse that tends slowly to "fade away" in spite of a ravenous appetite. Fortunately a simple test for this is available. Consumption in the horse is a disease of the belly or bones and not of the chest.

THE IDENTIFICATION OF HORSES AND PONIES

Breeds. Colours. Markings. Age. Height. Sex.

BREED

For a horse to be correctly described as belonging to a certain breed it is necessary that the horse in question shall be recorded in the Stud Register of the breed society concerned or have the right to be so recorded.

The following are some of the recognised breeds of light horses and ponies: Thoroughbreds, which figure in the General Stud Book; Hackneys; Cleveland Bays; Arabs and Anglo-Arabs; Shetland; New Forest; Dartmoor; Exmoor; Dales; Fell; Highland; Welsh and Connemara ponies. For all of these stud registers exist.

Half-breds

The term half-bred is used to denote a horse, one of whose parents is a thoroughbred.

Type

Hunters, hacks, polo ponies, cobs, and vanners are types of horse as distinct from breeds.

COLOUR

The deciding factor in assessing the colour of a horse or pony, particularly where doubt exists, lies in reference to the colour of the "points". Points, in this connection, are considered to be: the muzzle, tips of the ears, mane and tail and the extremities of the four legs. White in itself is not a colour, being merely the indication of lack of colour (pigmentation).

A *black* horse is black in colour with black points.

A *brown* horse is dark brown or nearly black in colour with brown points.

A *bay* horse is a brown-coloured horse with black points.

A *chestnut* horse is a ginger or reddish colour with a similar mane and tail. "Light", "dark" and "liver" chestnuts are variations met with.

A *grey* horse is one in which both white and black hairs occur throughout the coat. An "iron grey" is one in which black is pronounced. A "light grey" is one in which white hairs predominate. A "fleabitten grey" is one in which the dark hairs occur in tufts. A horse is never correctly described as a "white horse".

Dun horses vary from mouse colour to golden, generally have black points and show either "zebra" marks on the limbs or a "list", i.e. a dark line along the back.

Roan horses, which may be of a "strawberry" or "bay" or "blue" colour, show a mixture of chestnut or bay and white, or black and white hairs throughout the coat.

A *piebald* horse is one showing large irregular patches of black and white, i.e. black and white like a magpie.

A *skewbald* horse is one showing large irregular patches of white and any other colour except black.

Horses which conform to no fixed colour may correctly be described as "odd coloured". The term bay-brown is also permissible in a horse that appears to conform partly but not exactly to bay or brown.

MARKINGS
The head

A *star* is a white mark on the forehead.

A *stripe* is a narrow white mark down the face.

A *blaze* is a broad white mark down the face which extends over the bones of the nose.

A *white face* includes the forehead, eyes, the nose and part of the muzzle.

A *snip* is a white mark between the nostrils, which in some cases extends into the nostrils.

A *wall eye* is one which shows white or blue-white colouring in place of the normal colouration.

The legs

A *stocking* is a white leg extending as far as the knee or hock.

A *sock* involves the fetlock and part of the cannon region.

A *white* fetlock, white pastern, or white coronet involve the part named only.

The term *ermine* is employed where black spots occur on white.

BRANDS

Brand marks—generally indications of previous ownership—are often seen on the Welsh, New Forest, Dartmoor and Exmoor pony breeds, and frequently on horses imported from America and Australia.

Brands are generally placed either on the flat of the shoulder, the saddle region or the quarters.

AGE

The age of a horse is determined by reference to the front (incisor) teeth. There are six of these teeth in each jaw. A horse has two complete sets of these teeth, namely, the *milk* (or temporary) teeth, and the permanent teeth. The milk tooth is small and white, has a distinct neck and a short fang. The permanent tooth is of a browner yellowish colour, is much larger and has no distinct neck to it.

The changeover from milk to permanent teeth occurs at certain definite ages and the ageing of a horse is based mainly upon this fact combined with the following additional indications:—

At **one** year the horse looks young, has a fluffy tail and shows six new unworn milk teeth in each jaw.

At **two** the horse still looks young but has lost the fluffy hairs of the tail. The jaws still show a complete set of milk teeth but they are now worn.

At **three** the centre two milk teeth in each jaw have been replaced by permanent teeth which are larger and show a sharp edge.

At **four** two more milk teeth in each jaw have been replaced, namely, those lateral to the centre two.

At **five** the corner milk teeth have been shed and show as new shell-like teeth at the corners.

At **six** there is a "full mouth" but the corner teeth have lost their shell-like appearance.

At **seven** a hook appears on the top corner tooth. A similar hook may show at thirteen years of age which may lead to confusion.

At **eight** the hook has disappeared, the tables of the teeth show wear and the black hollow centres have disappeared.

From eight onwards there is no certainty although, among other things, an intimate knowledge of the changes in the outline of the "tables" of the teeth and slope of the jaws enables an opinion to be formed.

In the male a tush appears behind the corner incisor at four years of age.

Thoroughbred are aged from the 1st January: other horses, from the 1st April.

MEASUREMENT

Height

The standard of height measurement in the horse is the "hand", which is equivalent to four inches. Shetland ponies, however, are measured in inches.

Measurement is made from ground level to the highest point of the withers. For accuracy in measurement the following conditions must be fulfilled. The place chosen must be smooth and level. The horse must stand squarely on all four feet with the forefeet together. The head must be lowered so that the poll comes in line with the withers. A special "measuring stick" provided with a spirit level on the cross bar must be employed.

If the horse is shod at the time of measurement it is usual to allow half an inch off the recorded height for the shoes provided they are normal shoes, i.e. not racing plates.

Life measurement certificates are now granted subject to the following conditions: the horse must be six years of age or over. Measurement may only be made between 10th March and 30th September. The measurement must be taken by one of the officially appointed measurers on the panel of the Joint Measurement Scheme, and with the horse standing unshod.

Height measurement in the horse has many uses, viz. it forms part of the correct description of the horse; it provides for subdivision of horses into classes for show purposes; it is an indication of the size of a horse offered in a sale catalogue or the size of a horse desired by a purchaser. It serves as an indication for the size of clothing, saddlery or harness on purchase from a saddler.

Bone

This term is used in relation to measurement taken around the foreleg immediately below the knee. A hunter with "good bone" should measure $8\frac{1}{2}$ inches or more. Where the measurement falls short of requirements the horse is said to be "light of bone", indicating that his limbs are not up to the weight that his body should carry.

TERMS APPLIED TO HORSES AT VARIOUS AGES

At birth; a *foal*. If a male: a *colt foal;* if a female: a *filly foal;* both up to the 1st January following birth.

In the year after birth the term *yearling* is used.

In the second year after birth the term *two year-old* is used.

A *colt* is a young male up to 3 years of age.

A *filly* is a young female up to 3 years of age.

A *gelding* is a castrated male of any age.

An *entire* or *stallion* is an uncastrated male.

A *mare* is a female of any age.

It is not easy to define exactly the difference between a *horse* and a *pony*. It is by no means entirely a matter of height though normally horses measure over 15 hands. To a very large extent the difference lies in a matter of temperament.

A *cob* is a mare or gelding between 14-2 and 15-1 hands with a head and neck resembling a pony and the body and limbs of a horse.

A *mule* results from the cross between a donkey stallion and a pony mare. A *jennet* is the product of a pony stallion out of a she-ass.

How to describe a horse.

The following is an example of the full description of a pony:—

" 'Kitty', a brown registered New Forest pony mare, rising five years, 13-2 hands without shoes, with a star, snip into near nostril, coronet ermine near-fore, sock off-fore, pastern partly near-hind and a stocking off-hind. Scar near-hind cannon. Branded 'C.D.' near saddle. Mane and tail on."

TRANSPORTATION

So many ponies are now taken to shows and gymkhanas by horse trailers that a note on this subject will not be out of place.

Equipment

Headstalls should be worn in preference to halters, and they should be strong and well-fitting. The headrope may, with advantage, be slightly longer than the standard size to facilitate leading up the ramp. In some cases double head-ropes are desirable, one attached to each of the side "D's" of the headstall.

Knee caps to protect knees, and in some cases also hock boots to save the point of the hock from injury, ought to be regarded as essentials where valuable animals are concerned.

The tail requires protection by means of either a tail bandage or a special tail guard, otherwise disarrangement of hair, or an unsightly rub of the tail, may result.

The question of whether the pony is rugged or not depends upon what he is used to in the stable and upon weather conditions. A summer sheet with fillet strings or an anti-sweat rug, may be all that is necessary on a summer day. Rugs, whether worn or not, ought to be included with the equipment taken for use should the pony be overheated on leaving the ring.

Boxing

Transporters who own horse trailers are generally experienced in the loading of difficult ponies, and as a rule the task is better left to them. Many a pony that refuses to enter the box willingly can be induced to do so by loading his stable companion first of all. In extreme cases the one should follow up the ramp close on the heels of the other. The shy loader having ventured into the trailer should be rewarded at once by a handful of oats. Oats for this purpose should be on hand every time the pony is loaded until the pony has overcome all fear. When loading, all persons except the one leading the pony should be well behind the line of the ramp and the pony's quarters. Nothing stops the hesitating pony quicker than a person standing too far forward and staring at it or trying to steer with waving arms. Once loaded, ponies should be secured to a ring or bar with a normal length of rope, i.e. neither too long nor too short. A quick-release type of knot should be employed.

In cases of extreme difficulty in loading, the use of cavesson ropes is generally successful. It is as well to carry two of these in the box at all times in case of emergency. Attach one cavesson rope to each ramp rail. Lead the pony up to the ramp quietly and stand him straight, facing the ramp. Pass the loose ends of the ropes behind the pony, so that they cross just above the hocks. An assistant on each rope should gradually but firmly pull the ropes from the sides, so that they tighten behind the pony's quarter, while the pony is led up the ramp.

Watering and feeding

On a long expedition arrangements for watering and feeding while away from home are essential, but even on a short day, a bucket for water, and hay for the return journey ought to be taken. Hay is best transported ready loaded into hay nets and corn in a nosebag kept for the purpose tied up at the top when not in use.

Insurance

It is possible to take out a special policy of insurance for the show season to cover ponies against show and transportation risks. Most transporters, however, who have horse trailers for hire have a policy of their own which fully covers any animal against transit risks while using the vehicle.

Transport by air

Increasing use of this method is now being made particularly between Britain, Eire and the continent. However, not all horses travel well by air. A capable attendant able to deal with panic or fright must accompany the horse. Protective clothing should be provided particularly rugs, bandages, a tail guard and a poll pad. The last named is designed to protect the poll region from a blow when passing through a low doorway or under a low beam and to minimise the development of the injury known as poll evil which often follows a severe contusion there.

INDEX

NOTES

NOTES

NOTES

NOTES

NOTES

NOTES

NOTES

NOTES

OTHER OFFICIAL PUBLICATIONS

British Horse Society and Pony Club Publications

"THE INSTRUCTOR'S HANDBOOK OF THE BRITISH HORSE
SOCIETY AND THE PONY CLUB"

*"TRAINING THE YOUNG HORSE AND PONY"

"KEEPING A PONY AT GRASS" by Mrs. O. Faudel-Phillips, F.I.H.

"MOUNTED GAMES AND GYMKHANAS"

"CAMPING FOR THE PONY CLUB"

"A GUIDE TO THE PURCHASE OF CHILDREN'S PONIES"

"RIDING TO HOUNDS"

"NOTES FOR FIVE-MINUTE LECTURES—FOXHUNTING"

"THE PONY CLUB YEAR BOOK"

"BASIC TRAINING FOR YOUNG HORSES AND PONIES"
by Mrs. V. D. S. Williams

"THE FOOT AND SHOEING" by Major C. Davenport, F.R.C.V.S.

"THE GENERAL PURPOSE SEAT" by Col. The Hon. C. G.
Cubitt, D.S.O., T.D., D.L., and Col. G. T. Hurrell, O.B.E.

"BITS AND BITTING" by Col. The Hon. C. G. Cubitt

"THE AIDS AND THEIR APPLICATIONS" by Col. The Hon.
C. G. Cubitt, D.S.O., T.D., D.L.

(*Film Strips are also available for each of these titles*)

"THE PONY CLUB STANDARDS OF EFFICIENCY"

"THE PONY CLUB HUNTING AND COUNTRY LORE TESTS"

"RULES FOR DRESSAGE"

"RULES FOR COMBINED TRAINING"

*"RIDING" by Mrs. V. D. S. Williams (*Published for the British Horse
Society by Educational Productions Ltd.*)

An up-to-date list of publications is shown in the Pony Club Year
Book, issued annually. A list of books recommended for further
reading is maintained by the B.H.S.

These and other publications connected with the horse are available from

THE BRITISH HORSE SOCIETY
National Equestrian Centre
Kenilworth, Warwickshire, CV8 2LR

*These are available from

BARRON'S EDUCATIONAL SERIES, INC.

113 Crossways Park Drive

Woodbury, New York 11797